NORTH TO PARADISE

A MEMOIR

OUSMAN UMAR

TRANSLATED BY KEVIN GERRY DUNN

 AMAZON

T0002007

NORTH
TO
PARADISE

Previously published as *Viaje al país de los blancos* by PLAZA & JANES in Spain in 2019. Translated from Spanish by Kevin Gerry Dunn. First published in English by Amazon Crossing in 2022.

Published by Amazon Crossing, Seattle
www.apub.com

Amazon, the Amazon logo, and Amazon Crossing are trademarks of Amazon.com, Inc., or its affiliates.

ISBN-13: 9781542030113 (hardcover)
ISBN-10: 1542030110 (hardcover)
ISBN-13: 9781542030137 (paperback)
ISBN-10: 1542030137 (paperback)

Cover design by Rex Bonomelli

Printed in the United States of America

First edition

*For Musa, and for all those who lose their lives
every day as they journey to the Land of the Whites.*

*For my mother, who gave me the chance to be born
again, and for my father, who supported me every
step of the way.*

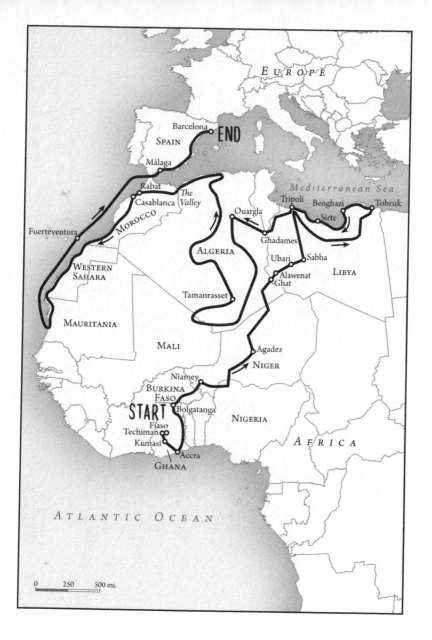

PROLOGUE

The desert is full of corpses, scattered among the dunes.

A man sat down. Alone. In the middle of the desert. We had been walking for days, trusting the man who said he could lead us out of those endless sands. We had no food or water. Hope dwindled with each passing day. There was nothing as far as the eye could see. The wind howled, and the air burned in our lungs.

That man, the man who sat down, couldn't go any farther. He had used his last ounce of strength.

"Leave me," he said.

He didn't care if he died.

"You can do it," we urged him. "Just hang on a little longer. We'll be there soon."

"Leave me," he repeated.

"There can't be much farther to go."

"Leave me."

"We're going to be all right, we're the chosen ones."

"Leave me . . ."

He just sat, alone, in the middle of the desert. Slowly, we started walking again. He got smaller and smaller until he disappeared. I imagined him dying silently, over the course of days, his last breath as feeble as a bird's. Then he must have lain there, dry and rigid, just like all the other bodies we'd encountered along the way.

The smugglers had abandoned us, betrayed us in the middle of nowhere, without explanation. We wanted to reach Paradise, the Promised Land. When we started out, there were forty-six of us. Only six survived.

HOME (GHANA)

I was born on a Tuesday. I don't know the month or the year because that doesn't matter in my tribe. But I know I was born in the tropical African country called Ghana. My village, in the Brong-Ahafo region, within the Techiman District, is in the middle of the jungle, surrounded by lush vegetation. It's an incredibly fertile region: drop a seed anywhere and a plant will grow. My mother died giving birth to me. According to the traditions of my tribe, the Wala, when this happens, the baby must be abandoned because it was born under a curse. It's left to die. Luckily, my father, Seidu, was a shaman from the tribe's royal family, and he could save me. Our distant ancestor founded the Kingdom of Wa, and his descendants became the four branches of the family—known as the four gates—that take turns governing. We belonged to one of those gates.

The Wala have their own unique form of identification: a small scar on the right cheek, a small cut we're given when we're born so we can recognize each other. It's important: in a fight, it may mean the difference between being taken down as an enemy or protected as a fellow tribesman.

As a shaman, my father was not a member of the Islamic faith. Though his wife and children were Muslim, he adhered to the religion of our ancestors. When his father died, the family performed a ritual and the spirits chose my father to continue the shamanic practice; the tradition has been passed down in this way for generations. My father believed that the gods are everywhere—in nature, in rivers and mountains—and that all things have a soul. Growing up, I was always confused because I shared his religion at home and the Muslim religion in the community. Even as a child, I could tell people thought of Islam and Christianity as somehow superior to the ancestral religion. My father wasn't even allowed in the mosque.

Being spared as a child was the first miracle I experienced in my life, the first of many times I narrowly escaped death. To save me, my father moved us to another village, Fiaso, where we lived with my aunt, the woman who raised me. I grew up thinking she was my mother, but she was actually my mother's sister.

In Fiaso, we spent our days working the fields. If we wanted to eat chicken, we grabbed one from the poultry yard. If we wanted to eat some other animal, we'd hunt it in the jungle. At night, we set traps, and as soon as dawn broke, we'd run out to see what we'd caught. And when there was nothing else, we'd gather mangos, oranges, and all the other things that nature provides. You never go hungry in the countryside. I had it easy in my village: I was the shaman's son, and I lived in a big house. I didn't think about my future much. I expected that my life would be typical: I would live off the earth, tend to the animals, marry, and have children.

The houses in my village were made of clay, and the roofs were made of bamboo, branches, and other plants. We took our water from the river. Actually, there were two rivers: one female and the other male. One was for drinking, the other for washing. I've never tasted such fresh, crystalline water anywhere else. There was no electricity, so we used kerosene. There was so little artificial light that at night, you could see millions of stars shining in the sky, like burning embers dotted across the heavens. When I was a boy, on nights with a full moon, the light was so strong we could play outside.

"If you stare at the moon too hard," the elder women told us, "a witch will come and kill you." They also warned us not to point at graveyards. That could kill you too—unless you swallowed a pebble first, of course.

It rained a lot in my village, and the houses were made from natural materials, so we had to make constant repairs. My father was very good at that kind of thing, and people always asked him to help mend or build houses, or oversee the work. That was another reason everyone respected him.

My father was a serious man with a slight build, and he was very agile. With us, his children, he was distant and severe, not talking much, except to give orders: "Come do this, go do that." He taught us not through words, but through actions, which we learned to imitate. I respected him immensely. My adopted mother, Amina, was cheerful and talkative. Besides managing domestic tasks, she also sold essential goods, like salt and peanuts, which she brought from the town of Techiman. My mother was kind, even when my father was strict. She always tried to shield us from his beatings. Once, I dropped the water gourd on the way back from the river and it broke. He became very angry and beat me badly. "Even if he kills me, it's not going to fix the shattered gourd," I remember thinking. "What's the point in getting so upset?" It's normal to beat children as punishment there.

I was a soccer fanatic, even though my father didn't approve. With my best friends, Francis, Jafaro, and Salu, I would set up a soccer field (though in Ghana, we call it football) in the flat areas outside the village. I played forward, and I was pretty good. My team always won. Francis could buy soccer balls in Techiman because his parents gave him an allowance, so he always brought the ball. Whenever he got mad, he'd grab the ball, say it was his, and leave us with no way to play. Sometimes I'd get so caught up playing soccer that I'd be late to tend the goats, which made my father furious. So it felt really special when one day, when we were playing a proper match rather than just a scrimmage, he came to watch me play. I remember playing better than I ever had before, knowing that he was watching and that he was proud of me. He was in shorts, but he also wore a beautiful green-and-yellow kente cloth that he saved for special occasions.

I lived with my extended family—there were twenty of us—in a big house with a central courtyard we used for meetings and household tasks, like preparing food or hanging up laundry to dry. Parents, grandparents, cousins, aunts, and uncles, we shared a strong bond. In my land, family is sacred, and elders are the most important and respected of all. Children are just work mules; nobody pays much attention to them. Elders are the wisest because they have lived the longest. Since knowledge is hard to come by, the best way to learn something is to ask an elder.

At night, around the fire, the elders would share their experiences and tell folktales where animals were the main characters. That was how we learned about nature and survival. I remember a story about a man-spider who was the wisest in his village. He wanted to make sure no one could ever be wiser than he was, so he tried to collect all the world's knowledge, put it in a gourd, and hang it from a tree where no one could ever reach it. He tried to climb the tree with the gourd hanging from his belly, but it was too heavy, so his son, Kuakuata, suggested carrying it on his back. This enraged the father because he realized he hadn't collected all the world's knowledge after all—his son knew something he didn't! The elders used that story to teach us that you can never know everything.

We had a special room in the house for my father's shamanic rituals. It was a sacred place: you could only go inside barefoot, as if it were a temple. People called on my father to perform divinations and healings, or call for rain or blessings on the earth to make it more fertile. Whenever someone came to him for a divination, he would drink a powerful liquor, draw a circle in ash on the ground, take a rooster (that I handed him), and slit its throat. Then he would summon those who had come before us: "Today, Father, Grandfathers, ancestors, we turn to you for help."

He would spill the blood on the altar, which was always covered in blood, feathers, and entrails from earlier rituals. Then he would put the rooster on the ground, and it would run around the room in a frenzy until it died. If it fell faceup, it meant the answer to the question was yes. Otherwise, it meant the question required further investigation, and my father would turn to his box of precious stones for a reading. People were always very grateful when they left.

My father could also cure snakebites with herbal remedies and the help of the ancestors. This was handy because there were a lot of snakes in the area. He was so famous that once, they tried to hire him at a hospital, but he preferred to stay in the village. My father never charged for his services.

"The gods have no price," he used to say.

Francis, Salu, Jafaro, and I often played together in the jungle. It was wonderful: we would run, climb trees, eat fruit, and hunt small animals with our slingshots. One of our favorite activities was catching birds. There were three kinds—reds, browns, and pios—and if you caught one and put it in a cage, it would attract others, which you could then also catch. Whoever caught the most birds was king of the village children, the most popular. We also had lots of fun building toys, like little cars and trucks. I was pretty good at that too.

Once, I went to set bird traps in the jungle alone. I'd made a cage with a revolving door, and I put a little food inside as bait. I also placed a bird I'd caught earlier in the cage and added pepper to its water so it would sing more and attract its friends. Then I hid in the bushes so the birds wouldn't be afraid to approach. After a while, I realized the caged bird was singing more than usual. When I came out of my hiding place to see why, I saw a snake circling the cage, looking for a way in so it could capture the bird. I was so scared I ran away, but when I looked back, I was surprised to see that the snake was fleeing too, in the opposite direction. That day I learned that we're all afraid of the unknown.

—◊—

I remember the day a strange machine crossed the sky. I stared, astonished; I'd never seen anything like it. It looked like a bird, but it flew very high, and very straight, and left two trails of white smoke behind it.

"What is that?" I asked the elders. "Is it magic?"

"It's an airplane," I was told. "White men build them, and white men fly them."

They didn't offer more of an explanation than that because elders had better things to do than spend all day answering children's questions.

My village is in a remote region of Ghana, and Ghana itself is remote relative to the Land of the Whites. The elders said the whites lived very far away, that they lived like gods, and they were all pilots, engineers, doctors . . . I wanted that to be me, I wanted to be white. I watched planes plow across the African sky, and listened to stories about the whites: strange, terrifying, wondrous stories.

We got a tiny glimpse into that world once a month, when almost everyone in Fiaso gathered together to watch a movie in the village square. We kids thought movies were white people's magic and even tried to jump into the movie through the screen. We didn't succeed. They always showed action movies, often the same few Arnold Schwarzenegger films. He was very strong and killed everyone, which made us think the white man was some kind of violent, superhuman creature. The bad guys were Japanese, and always seemed really stupid: they'd just stand around in a line, so when Schwarzenegger jumped out of the bushes, it was easy for him to mow them down with one burst from his machine gun. He didn't even think twice.

Once, Catholic priests came and showed a movie about Jesus Christ. It was a tragic day: a drunk villager had parked his tractor without remembering the hand brake, and it rolled down an embankment into the village square, where we were all engrossed in the movie. Three people were killed.

As a kid, I thought movies were real, that it was all true. When I learned the characters were actors, I was very upset. How could they pretend like that? They were imposters! How could you trust people who pretended to cry, who pretended to be happy?

We didn't have much in the way of material goods—we wore several pants at once to cover each pair's holes—and seeing the white people's movies made us long for things we couldn't afford but didn't need. If you don't know something exists, you can't want it. But you also can't try to shield rural Africans from all the material things the world has to offer. It's not possible, and it's not right.

Looking back on my childhood, I can see these lofty ideas about white people and Europe seem absurd because of course talent, intelligence, and strength have no color. But these attitudes didn't take shape overnight: they are the product of centuries of enslavement, exploitation, colonialism, and what ultimately amounts to a white-supremacist marketing campaign to convince Black people to undervalue their own worth.

But I knew none of that back then, and I had no reason to expect my life to be different from anyone else's in my village, toiling in the sun and living in a mud house. I did have a premonition, though, which I didn't understand until years later. In our traditions, dreams are very important. I dreamed I was walking along a road that crossed a deep jungle. Toward the end of the dream, the road began to ascend a very tall mountain on the horizon, though there are no mountains in my region. It was a sad dream: in it, my father had died. But beyond that mysterious mountain, the sun was beating down. Its powerful red rays lit my face. It felt like something was calling me.

—⚋—

Because I was good at building toy cars, people always told my father, "Your boy Ousman is handy. You should send him to town to learn a trade."

"He will. I'll send him one day," he would reply.

My father was a stern man. As I said, he didn't ask for things; he gave orders. So when he told me I would go to the closest town, Techiman, to be an apprentice, it wasn't a suggestion. I would work at an auto body shop that belonged to an uncle on my mother's side (in Ghana, we call this being a panel beater). I loved the idea—I was very curious about the world. Soon after, I left home with a black plastic garbage bag that contained all my worldly possessions: four T-shirts and little else. I was around nine years old. I took a trotro (a minibus that leaves only once it's full) to my uncle's workshop, eighteen kilometers away. I didn't miss my family, and didn't think about them much, but being on my own felt odd: I was used to spending time with my siblings and taking care of them when my mother was working in the fields.

When I got to the door, I couldn't bring myself to go inside. I was so nervous that I walked in circles around the workshop, afraid to enter or even knock on the door. The entire time, my aunt (whom I'd never met before) was watching me from a window without my realizing it. Eventually she opened the door and called out, "What are you doing? Are you ever going to come in?" I was just a kid, and I was so embarrassed.

Techiman struck me as the most beautiful city in the world, as magnificent as I imagined New York City to be. I felt small there. It had everything: houses, shops, markets. People were always well dressed, and the roads were even paved! It made walking in the rain possible, unlike in my village, where everything turned into mud under the downpours. The smell of the rain-soaked roads of Techiman is still etched in my mind. It wasn't necessarily a pleasant aroma, it's a very specific smell, like burning metal, but there is still something special about it to me. On weekends when I was allowed to visit my village, I'd put on airs, as if I'd seen everything, the little kid back from the big city.

"Can you do the seven on airplanes?" a friend asked on one of my visits home.

In Ghana, holding your arm out the window while driving a car is called "doing the seven." Symbolically, it means things are going well for you: having a car was like achieving the American dream. A luxury. When I went back to my village, I'd always get questions like that, since I'd been around the world. But they'd also fill me in on the village rumors:

"The whites are so strict that if you marry a white lady and then cheat on her, she'll kill you, because white people all have guns."

—◆—

Workshops in Ghana operate in a very particular way: the first boy to join as an apprentice is the most senior, and each new apprentice is less important than the one before. If you're the newest, or "last boy," you have it the worst. You're the first to arrive in the morning to sweep everything, clean, and prepare the tools, you're the one they send on errands at all hours, and you're the last to shower and leave. You eat what is left over from your boss's meal and always go a little hungry. That's how it goes until a new boy joins and you move up a rung on the ladder. But I never got to move up a rung because I left before any other boys joined.

My uncle traded in windshields, and he'd send me out to hawk them on the street. But I wanted to learn more about auto bodywork and hone my skills. That was why I'd left my village. I was talented and I learned fast, but hanging around on the roadside was getting in the way of my training. Nine months after I arrived, I left the workshop. A boy in my village had told me about his work in Kumasi, the second-largest city in Ghana; he said tips were good there. So when a truck came to pick up yuccas and yams from the village, I asked for a ride. My friend was learning to be a mechanic, and he helped me get a job in an auto repair shop.

In Kumasi, people mostly slept in workshops or street markets—wherever they could. Renting a room is a sign of some economic success. I slept in the shop where I worked, but I made friends with a boy whose mother was a trader. That meant she spent a lot of time outside the city, in other countries, so sometimes I could use a room in the Tafo neighborhood, where there were a lot of trotros.

The poorest boys, the ones who live on the street and don't have anything to do, travel with the trotro drivers. It's their job to call out the minibus's destination as it passes potential passengers on the street. Over time, they learn the job, so one day they can have their own trotro. This means most trotro drivers actually come from the poorest families, families that sleep on the street. They're a savvy bunch. Baba, who was also from my village, was one of these boys. I met him first in the

Tafo neighborhood. I was interested in learning what he did, because with a job like that, at least you don't go hungry. You get to eat every day.

"Look at you, Baba," I said. "You already have life all figured out."

"Well, you can come help out in the afternoons," he replied.

So some days, after work (always late because there are no fixed schedules, you work as long as there's something to do), I'd wait for Baba by the roadside and ride with him for the last two or three trips of the day. Around midnight, when we finished, we'd clean the minibus and he'd invite me to have dinner with him. I always ate as much as I could because I knew it might be days before I'd have another meal.

Through Baba I met Musa, a boy from Kumasi. We'd all clean the trotro and eat together. On weekends, we went for walks because they knew their way around the neighborhood. Musa was a little older and stockier than I was. He had a unique personality: At first, he seemed serious and guarded. But eventually I saw what a sweet, relaxed person he was. He didn't have a wicked bone in his body: he was peaceful and he didn't like conflict. I never argued with him—I doubt it would even have been possible. His family was poor, all sharing one rented room. Together, Musa and I fantasized for the first time about going to Libya to earn a living.

He talked a lot about the girl he was in love with. Her father owned a well, and we'd always say we were thirsty so we'd have an excuse to catch a glimpse of her, no matter how brief. If you liked a girl, you had to hang around her house, like you just happened to be passing by, looking for some excuse to talk to her. Or you had to ask your friend to tell her you wanted to talk—it was a pretty elaborate ritual. Being a girl's boyfriend just meant having a special friendship with the girl, spending more time with her. Nothing beyond that. Although many of those special friendships led to a wedding.

"When my journey is over, I'll come back to Ghana for her," Musa would say, even though his journey had not even begun.

—✺—

The first time my father spoke to me like an adult was during that period, when I was back from Kumasi for a visit. While we were working in the fields, he asked how I was faring in the city. He talked about personal topics—how he had separated from my mother, who had gone to her village in the north with two of my siblings. This was unusual: in Ghana, when parents separate, the children usually stay with the father, as if they were his property. I was surprised to hear my father talking to me like this: he already considered me an adult.

As the ground dried up in the winter, so did work in Kumasi: the demand for labor always drops substantially during the dry season. If there's no work, there are no tips, and if there are no tips, there's no food, so I was having a rough time of it. I'd made friends with my boss, and he gave me good tips because he saw I was genuinely invested in my job. But without work, his generosity didn't help much. A friend told me there was a lot of work in Accra, specifically Tema Harbor, the most important port in the country. And it was true; it was a good place to earn money: there were always lots of trucks driving through to pick up goods. When they broke down, they'd pay triple for repairs. This friend offered to take me with him, saying he was going to open a mechanic's shop. But I felt guilty about leaving my boss, who had treated me so well and even forgiven some debts I owed him, so I stayed.

My friend came back the next week full of optimism about Accra, promising I'd have it good at the harbor, telling me there was more work than I would know what to do with. He painted a rosy picture and talked me into it. I left, just for a week to earn a little cash. But I felt guilty, so I lied to my boss, saying I was returning to my village to ask my father for some food and money. I hadn't counted on the fact that many of the truckers who drive through Tema also drive through Kumasi. They pick up their cargo at the harbor (cement, salt, etc.) and haul it inland. After I'd been there just a few days, I received a message from my boss. Some truckers had seen me there and told my boss, "Hey, we saw your boy, what's his name? Ousman? He's working at Tema."

My boss sent a messenger asking me to come back, saying he wasn't upset, I could come back to work, it was no big deal. But I was too ashamed, and so I never went back to that mechanic's shop in Kumasi.

—◆◆◆—

The world was growing with me. When I lived in my village, I thought my village was the world. When I traveled to Techiman, I realized that the world was just a bit bigger. Then, in Kumasi, the world grew even more. And then, at the port of Accra, I set eyes on the sea for the first time. It was so blue, so immense, I didn't know where it ended. It terrified me, but still, I dreamed that there, just on the other side of the waves, was Paradise. I didn't have any idea what the world was like. I didn't know which sea it was. I didn't even know how to read or how to interpret a map. It was there that the idea of leaving Africa and traveling to the Land of the Whites truly began to take shape.

I didn't like Accra much. There was a lot of traffic, a lot of hustle and bustle. It was impressive, though. But at Tema Harbor, my fascination with the Land of the Whites continued to grow: ships arrived from that mysterious country full of wondrous cargo. Fantastical cars (they were actually used cars, but to us they were new), TV sets, secondhand computers . . . The abundance of goods produced outside of Ghana, used outside of Ghana, and then, when no one wants them anymore, sold in Ghana.

"Every year, the whites throw everything out and buy all new things," a friend told me. "That's how rich they are. They live in the lap of luxury. Everything that comes through the port is stuff they don't want."

"How could they not want these treasures?" I replied, watching the ships being unloaded.

The barges arrived bursting with riches. Thieves hung around the port, waiting to break into the containers and take what they could to sell it on the cheap: there were always people on the street hawking CD and DVD players, bikes, and so on. Whenever a car came off a ship, we'd jostle to get a chance to touch it: we wanted to feel and smell the white dust from Paradise—we loved the smell of Paradise. It was there, in Accra, that I watched television for the first time; I'd only ever seen movies projected onto a screen before. The TVs were supposed to be loaded onto enormous trucks for distribution, but one night, someone managed to get one working. We all crowded together to watch it. This was the first time I ever saw a working television, and they were showing a soccer game. Barça was playing. I had never heard of Barcelona before—in fact, that was the first time I ever heard of Spain at all. Looking at the TV set, I finally understood that it was a machine, not some magical object. It was such a shocking revelation that, to this day, I can't see a Barça jersey without remembering that feeling.

I led an austere life repairing big trucks. The other boys working there and I didn't have anywhere to live, so we slept in the trucks: one truck tonight, another truck tomorrow night. I was a twelve-year-old kid living in a no-man's-land between the port, the cement factory, and the fishing harbor. It was full of scrap and debris, a dumping site lousy with mosquitos. Somehow, though, I never got malaria; I didn't even know what it was to be afraid of it. In my village, people went to the healer more than the doctor. For example, I think my adopted mother died of cancer, but she thought it was witchcraft. She was in the hospital for two months, but she left because she insisted she was bewitched, not sick. These beliefs have deep roots.

At one point in Tema, while I was working on a welding project, there was a terrible accident. The valve that connected the torch to the acetylene tank wasn't properly closed, and gas had been escaping. I turned slightly, and the flame ignited the gas, causing a small explosion that burned half of my face. For two weeks, I couldn't see anything out of my left eye, just haze. I still have the scar above my left eyebrow—my welding degree.

This was one of the many times I narrowly escaped death. The working conditions in Ghana are very poor. No one cares about their workers' safety, and there are no laws. It's the sketchiest situation imaginable. We spent every day cutting huge sheets of metal with no protective gear, not even shoes, facing danger day in and day out. And we were all ages: there are no restrictions. There are many industries that exploit child labor in brutal conditions, but this isn't always the case; many families rely on their children to help work in the fields, as I had when I was still in Fiaso. This kind of work is an integral part of the culture, and it's not considered abusive.

I dreamed about crossing the sea and finding Paradise, where I wouldn't have to spend my days working outdoors. But my friends said that I should go to Libya, where I could find work and earn a monthly salary.

The same set of truckers usually passed through Tema, and we would always chat. I remember once, when I was cleaning up after doing repairs for a trucker I knew well—and who had been to Libya—he told me I could build a better life there: "With expertise and skills like yours, you'll get a job there, no problem," he assured me. "They'll even pay you a decent salary."

That's how information circulates at the port: people swap stories, and information travels by word of mouth. My face lit up. I had never had a fixed salary before, just whatever tips and food my bosses gave me. The trucker transported salt to Niger; I'd met him first when I fixed his truck at the port. We became friends, and in Africa, when you befriend someone older, they look out for you. For example, he always paid for my food when we ate together. He could take me to Niamey, the capital of Niger, and from there, I could continue my journey to Libya by bus. First, though, I would talk it over with my father.

I was always happy to go back to visit my village—I remember feeling excited on the trotro ride from Accra. Being back in Fiaso again meant seeing my family and friends, who were always eager to hear stories from my adventures in the capital. This time, though, was going to be different.

Shortly after I arrived home, my father summoned me to his room and announced, "I've found a good girl for you, from a good family. You'll marry. Soon you will have to ask for her hand. You will have a future here. You will build a family."

It felt like I couldn't say no, but I'd already acquired a Yellow Card, a certificate that says you don't have yellow fever, which is required for travel.

"It's still early," I told my father. "We'll see. I might leave the country. But I don't know when yet."

He nodded somberly. He was silent for a long while. "Son, if you're thinking of doing this, there's something important for you to know." He was clearly uncomfortable; this was a topic he didn't want to discuss. Eventually, he explained that the woman who had raised me—who I'd grown up calling my mother—was actually my aunt. I hadn't known until then. Where I come from, these kinds of things are taboo; you simply don't talk about them. I was utterly devastated by the news: that last time I left my house, I was crying so hard my siblings walked with me to the trotro stop, trying to console me. I felt like my whole life had been a lie. I wanted to disappear. Even though I had already been considering it, you could say that, in some sense, this pushed me to finally leave for Libya. I never saw my father again.

TOGO, BURKINA FASO, NIGER

I watched the trees fly by. I'd try to focus on one as we sped past it, then another. It was hard to keep my eyes on them because they vanished in the blink of an eye. I liked to pretend that the truck was standing still and that the world, with its trees, was rushing past. First I'd watch the closest trees, which were gone in an instant; then I'd try with the trees in the distance, which moved slowly on the edge of the horizon before disappearing. To stave off boredom, I focused on the trees and my goal: arriving in Libya, getting a good job, and traveling to the Land of the Whites.

We had just set off from Kumasi, where I met my trucker friend. The salt truck was enormous, and the driver traveled with two assistants, who did maintenance work, like changing the tires and fixing the engine if necessary. If you have car trouble in Ghana, you've got to jury-rig things as best you can, wherever your vehicle breaks down. Assistants pay the driver during their apprenticeship in the hope that, over time, they'll learn the trade and eventually have their own truck. Our freight was so heavy that the truck couldn't go very fast, and the trip took several weeks. On these long-haul freight trips, the driver sleeps inside the truck, where there's a small space for a mattress in the cab behind the seats. Everyone else lays mats on the ground under the truck. That's where the assistants and I slept. At times, I had to hide behind the tons of salt in the back to avoid detection, since I didn't have papers; other times, I had to get out of the truck and walk through the night, and the driver picked me up on the other side of the border.

We had a few setbacks, like when we got to Bolgatanga, the capital of the Ghana's Upper East Region and home of the Frafra people, who do the lowest-paying jobs in the country. We had a serious breakdown there, and we had to wait two days for mechanics to arrive from Kumasi. I didn't know how we were going to fix the truck or how long the mechanics would take, and I worried that things might take a turn for the worse. What if we couldn't repair the truck? My journey had only just begun—was it already over? The uncertainty had me on edge, but everything turned out all right in the end. We continued on our journey from the jungle of Ghana to the desert territories of Niger, by way of Burkina Faso. There, I saw lots of poverty: when we stopped to buy rice, groups of desperate children would appear and try to steal it.

The biggest challenge might have been the one inside my own head: keeping your mind occupied during such a long, monotonous drive isn't easy. I spent countless hours drowsily watching the landscape and playing mental games with the trees. There weren't many other forms of entertainment. But even the trees became fewer and smaller as the climate changed around us: slowly but surely, the landscape shifted into harsh desert. Sand, sand, sand. I had no idea that entering the desert was like passing from life into death.

Despite everything, the first stage of my journey wasn't too rough. My concept of time was entirely different: if you had asked me what I would be doing five years in the future, I wouldn't have known. Long-term planning wasn't a priority; my concern was what I would eat that day and whether I'd have anything to eat the next. In Ghana, buses depart only when they're full; there's no hurry, and people wait patiently until all the seats are taken. You can't make many plans. And so, after a length of time that I can't quantify, we finally arrived in Niamey.

—◊◊◊—

Our trip ended at a huge truck stop. It was full of people in transit leaning against trucks and chatting, taking in some fresh air. They came from all over. When we arrived, I started talking to other truckers' assistants and travelers in Hausa, which is similar to Arabic and a kind of lingua franca spoken in much of West Africa.

"You've got to go to Agadez," they told me.

But how was I supposed to get there? Everyone made their own suggestions, and I pieced together that I had to find the minibus station and set out for Agadez from there. I joined a group of six others en route to Libya, and together we waited at the station for almost a whole day, swapping stories and insights. You've got to be careful around the people you meet; if you're too trusting, they might steal your money. That's why it's important to always keep it carefully hidden, especially while you're sleeping.

Finally, we got on the minibus for Agadez, and the journey continued. As the bus was approaching the city, we were stopped at a military checkpoint. We were forced off the bus and made to line up. A military official grabbed a fistful of sand, and we watched as it sifted through his fingers.

"Is this the sand from your country?" he asked.

"No."

"Then you've got to pay to set foot on it."

Without waiting for a response, the officials began to beat the strongest person in our group, to teach the rest of us a lesson. And it worked, we paid what they asked. Meanwhile, our driver, accustomed to these extortions, had decided to leave us there so he wouldn't fall behind schedule. We walked the final two hours to the city.

—⁓—

Agadez is a hostile and arid place. Short brown buildings stand between suffocating, narrow, labyrinthine streets where the locals set up markets. In the middle of the Nigerien desert, it's the start of what migrants call the "path through hell." That's where I was headed. The first hurdle on the route to Europe, through the desert in the hands of smugglers, often culminating in nameless, faceless death. The border between Niger and Libya is known as "the snakebite" because if anything happens to you there, you're a goner. It's perhaps the most desolate border in the world, a silent place in the desert, entirely uninhabited without so much as a road. It couldn't be more different from my home in the Ghanaian jungle, lush with vegetation and life: no, Agadez was a dead place. But human beings find ways to live in the least likely places, under the most adverse conditions.

Agadez is a converging point for migrants from several countries to the south, like a bottleneck. It's a bustling city, with people coming and going, kicking up dust in the streets. For centuries, it has been an important city for the Tuareg people because it is a major hub for caravans crossing the Sahara. Other travelers had told me to go straight to the main square when I arrived. There, I saw people loading large, seventies-era trucks until they were so heavily laden with people and cargo that it looked as if they might collapse at any moment. The passengers, bags, and jugs of water and gasoline hung off the sides, as uncomfortable and unstable as you can imagine. The journey in these subhuman conditions could last as long as two weeks. The consensus was that if one of these trucks broke down in the middle of the desert, there was no way to make repairs—that's it, end of story. A rescue was unthinkable.

"They've found trucks in the desert with eighty bodies around them," I overheard as I watched them loading the convoys.

Agadez is the unwitting home of many "sinkers," migrants who ran out of money. They can't afford to continue, and they can't afford to go home: stuck forever, like ghosts. I saw them everywhere. They live in extreme poverty and survive by finding clientele for the smugglers: they try to convince you to cross the desert with them. I'd been warned to walk around the city before making a decision, to think it over carefully. Find the best option. Some people aren't trustworthy. As I walked, I was approached by a tall, bearded Arab man in a robe. He was a Muslim, and he started talking to me about God. After a while, he offered me a different route to Libya:

"If you come with us in our Land Rover, you'll be much more comfortable. And it'll only take three days."

He was asking twice as much as a smuggler would charge to take you in a truck, but I still had some money. Not to mention, I didn't know how to read maps or judge distances. So after spending the whole day walking in circles, I decided to take him up on it. He was a man of God; he wouldn't trick me. I thought traveling with him would be easier, more like a taxi ride.

"Okay," I agreed. "I'll cross the desert with you."

Other men dressed similarly collected my fee, took me to a house on the edge of town, and locked me in with several other travelers. Suddenly, we were prisoners; we weren't allowed to leave. The place was full of flies. I tried to swat them away at first, but after a while, I got used to them crawling all over my face and arms. It didn't matter. The men gave us bread and water. We were there for a week. Eventually, there were over forty people in the house. "How will they fit all of us in the Land Rovers?" I wondered.

One day, as the door opened—like it did every few hours—and several travelers came in, I thought I recognized a face. The sun was behind them, and it was hard to tell, but I jumped up: it was Musa, my good friend Musa.

"Musa? What are you doing here?!"

"Ousman! It's you! I'm going to Europe too. Now we can travel together."

We bumped fists and hugged—our usual greeting—and talked about how we'd ended up in Agadez. I was glad to have a friend because the isolation can be immense on the journey north. It's just you, alone in the whole world, far from your family and friends, unable to contact them. Having someone trustworthy on the trip with you is important. Someone to commiserate with. Someone who could end up holding your life in their hands.

One Friday afternoon, just after prayers started, we were told it was time to leave. They packed forty-six men and boys into three cars like sardines. Each of us had brought a five-liter jug of water, wrapped up tight so it wouldn't get hot, plus a little bread and some cookies. With no other supplies, we set out for the desert sands.

—⁂—

The smugglers sped past checkpoints to avoid being stopped, because our expedition was illegal. We didn't have papers; even within Africa, we were undocumented immigrants. We had left at midday on Friday, in the middle of prayers, which increased the likelihood that checkpoints would be unattended. After five or six hours, we stopped somewhere in the middle of the desert. The smugglers told us to wait while they went looking for water and gasoline. This seemed strange, but we stayed, waiting, waiting, waiting . . . until a whole day had passed. No one came back for us.

When the sun rose the next day, one man in the group stood up:

"I know the way to Libya," he said. "It's that direction. I'm going to walk. If anyone wants to walk with me, come on."

How did he know the way? He was the only person in the entire group who had North African features; the rest of us were from tropical Africa. He was Black like we were, but lighter skinned, taller, more slender. We exchanged looks with one another as we noticed this difference for the first time. He seemed trustworthy. One by one, we all rose to follow him, including Musa and me. We became a procession of tiny specks crossing that vast, arid region. The smugglers' cruel business consisted of promising to bring people across the Sahara, collecting their fees, and then abandoning them in the middle of nowhere. Murder on a massive scale.

Abandoned in the desert, with no idea where I was and only one jug of water, I focused on the end of the journey. I tried not to lose hope and remembered a popular mantra from my country: "Forward ever, backward never." I took refuge in that sentence. Just keep moving forward, without indulging negative thoughts.

When the man realized we were all following him, he turned around:

"Hang on a second," he said. "I'm not showing you the way to Libya for free."

Everything operates on money—even in those desperate circumstances, it won out over human kindness. That man leveraged his knowledge of the desert to empty our pockets of the few coins we had left. He demanded more money from us every two days.

The first time we encountered human remains in the desert, we were horrified. They lay on the sand in the middle of nowhere, under the boundless sky. From afar, they were just unmoving dots on the sand. As we got closer, we saw that it was nine people, their bodies rigid and dry. We took their passports and the rest of their belongings, then buried them.

Who were these people? Who loved them? Who was waiting for news from them? Where? Now they were just anonymous corpses in the desert, their final resting place. Ever the optimist, I thought we were lucky because we hadn't met the same fate. We were going to reach our destination. I was still young, I must have been around thirteen, and I was used to doing whatever adults told me. Still, I felt like we were some kind of heroes, that we would emerge from our struggles victorious. Maybe it's because I was just a kid, but for some reason, I thought our chances were good. For the first few days, I wasn't afraid at all. The fear came later.

When we had used up our jugs, our priority quickly became finding water to survive. But valley after valley, everything was dry.

"We'll find water tomorrow for sure," Musa and I reassured each other.

At one point, we found a drinking well for goats: the water was contaminated with their excrement, but we drank it anyway. Considering the things we ate and drank, I don't know how we never got sick.

Whenever we were lucky enough to find moist sand, we grabbed fistfuls of it and squeezed it until a single drop fell on our lips. Other times, we couldn't even get that much; it was maddening. That was how we drank, drop by drop, each of those drops essential to our survival. Thanks to those tiny servings of water, we lived a few more hours and continued our journey. We ate garri, a typical Ghanaian food, a kind of dry paste you mix with a little bit of water. We had powdered milk, a few cookies, and hard bread. We pooled our food so that everyone could eat, if you can call that eating.

Day after day, we walked until we couldn't take another step, then looked for somewhere to spend the night. At dawn, we'd resume our journey, another day of walking. We rarely spoke: everyone was in his own head, immersed in his own thoughts. We were silent, like frontline soldiers focused on their targets. The difference in temperature between day and night was brutal: we practically melted during the day, when it was over 120 degrees Fahrenheit, but at night, it dropped to around 50, and we had to bury ourselves in the sand to keep warm.

Walk, that's all we did. Eventually, we had to make the grueling journey over the Hoggar Mountains. When we encountered another set of bodies, I started to realize that the desert was like a mass grave for migrants on their way to a better life.

The mountains were pure rock: it felt like if you removed a single stone, it would set off an avalanche and crush us. The ascent was difficult: it wasn't a question of walking up the mountain, but of scaling it, step by step, rock by rock, looking for a passage through wherever you could, often retracing your steps, with your body in a constant state of tension. The mountain seemed to go on forever; we climbed and climbed, and it remained before us, indifferent to our efforts. It was during that ascent that I began to be plagued by more somber thoughts. We had been walking for seven days, maybe ten, and I was beginning to think that maybe we wouldn't make it out alive. With every new stage of the journey, I lost a little more hope.

—⁓⁓—

The desert is not a homogenous place: sometimes it's sand dunes, sometimes it's rocky flatlands, and sometimes it's mountains and hills. From a distance, the desert seems monotonous, but as soon as you start walking, you see that it's quite varied. When we'd finally made it through the mountains and found some water, our spirits improved a bit. The terrain leveled out, and flat land felt like a walk in the park. We arrived at a beautiful spot with very tall stone walls—it looked as if it had been made by human hands, but it was a natural structure created by the wind. We were walking along the borders of Algeria, Niger, and Mali. We found water at the bottom of a deep cleft in the rock walls, surrounded by smooth stones. At last, water, all the cool water we wanted! We drank and washed; then we slept in that place, finally able to relax.

It got pretty cold, so I curled up in a stone nook and fell asleep there. The next morning, everyone woke up and began preparing to leave. They nearly started walking without me, but thankfully, one man came to relieve himself near where I was sleeping. His piss splashed off a rock and onto my sleeping body, and I woke up.

"What are you doing alone down there?" he asked. "Why did you leave the group? Come on, we're about to go!"

If it hadn't been for that lucky coincidence, I would have been left behind, and who knows what would have become of me. Everyone else was already in a line, ready to start walking.

The next few days were unspeakably painful. We had no food or water. We had to drink our own urine, but we were so desperate we didn't care. One man's feet were badly swollen and his shoes were falling apart; he had to use strings to hold them together. The sand is burning hot during the day and walking barefoot isn't an option. Survival seems impossible in these conditions, but when we encounter physical challenges, our bodies adapt in astonishing ways. The man with the swollen feet was the first to choose to die—he was the one who sat down in the sand, alone, waiting for the end. He couldn't bring himself to walk any farther, and he gave up: his fatigue and despair had become so great that he preferred a slow, certain, agonizing death.

We left him sitting there, and his figure receded behind us, as if the Sahara were swallowing him up, as if the desert were an enormous monster whose belly was full of the dead. I didn't want to think about his final hours. He wasn't the only one. When a member of the group died or told us to leave them, things changed. Our spirits fell. Musa and I tried to cheer each other up:

"The fact that we're still alive is a good sign," Musa would say.

"Yeah, we'll make it to Libya for sure," I'd answer.

"Once we're there, I swear, I'm never setting foot in the desert again."

Truth be told, we were all frightened, but nobody wanted to say it out loud since it would just feed our despair. How had we ended up in this inferno? We had no choice but to carry on. So we continued, until, one day, we decided to kill our guide.

Maybe it was a decision born of desperation: every day, he told us we had only one or two days to go, but then he'd say it again. The journey never ended. There was always farther to go. Eventually, he became a target of suspicion among the group. Why was he the only one who knew the way? At first, we thought he was like us, another migrant who wanted to go to Libya. But the longer our trek lasted, the less sure we became. Doubt had infected the group.

"What if he's with the smugglers?" someone suggested.

"How did he know the smugglers wouldn't come back with their Land Rovers?" another asked.

"Why does he keep asking for money?"

After many short, hushed conversations like these, we truly believed our guide was in league with the smugglers, working with them to squeeze every last penny out of us. Or at least, that's how it seemed at the time, based on the evidence available. Granted, it seemed insane to think that he'd risk his life and undertake this hellish journey under the burning sun just for money. But he was North African, probably Sahrawi, and used to living in these conditions, in a hut in the middle of the desert. It wouldn't have been as arduous for him as it was for us. He was familiar with the region and the climate, and his body was adapted to it. There are people who can survive for a full day on just one drop of water.

"We have to kill him," several members of the group declared.

I was a child, so I wasn't part of big decisions like this. But the adults had made up their minds: it was time to eliminate him.

The atmosphere within the group became strained; you could feel the tension as we trudged through the desert, staring at our feet. I think the guide could tell that a mutiny was brewing against him. Our prospects weren't good: we knew that if we killed our guide, our own deaths were all but certain. But we wanted to make sure he died first, so he wouldn't survive to lure other migrants into his trap. We would sacrifice our lives to save future victims from his deadly scam. We would sacrifice our lives to stop the suffering. That said, killing a man is no easy task, especially if you have to do it with your bare hands.

At the agreed-upon time, on the nineteenth day of our journey, we tried to jump him and beat him to death. But as soon as he detected the attack, he pulled out a knife and stabbed the first attacker. The man began bleeding heavily. After so much time in the desert, we were too weak to outmaneuver our guide, who screamed that he would kill anyone who came close. He wasn't bluffing. He'd entered a violent rage, and we didn't know what he was capable of. He had thwarted our attack, saved his own skin, and escaped.

—w—

After our guide ran off, the situation went from bad to worse. We were completely lost. Members of our group were passing out left and right, and all we could do was tell them to hang in there. Before long, we passed another set of bodies: one of them, wearing denim, had a canteen on him. I don't know why I thought to check it, but surprisingly, there was a little bit of liquid left, water or urine, I couldn't say. I felt guilty because in Muslim culture, stealing is wicked, even if it's from a dead person who doesn't need material things. Musa was the only one I told. I didn't know it then, but those few drops would save my life.

Not everyone had my luck. Many gave up and let death take them. Our group stopped walking—most had no strength left, and with no guide, they saw no point in fighting. They had reached their end. But Musa and I, along with four others, decided to continue. We still had a shred of hope, so we kept walking in the direction the guide had shown us before we tried to kill him.

"Are we even heading in the right direction?" I asked. "Or was he trying to trick us?"

"If we wait for nightfall, we might be able to see lights in the distance. That way we'll know if it's the right way," Musa reasoned.

So we did, but there were no lights. Even so, we kept walking for lack of an alternative. We agreed to continue as far as our strength would take us. My lips were so dry they split open every time I opened my mouth. I finally drank the liquid from the dead man's canteen, and that's what saved me. Three days after leaving the group, we saw vertical sticks in the distance.

"Do you see those sticks?" I asked the others. "Do you think they're electric poles?"

"I can't tell," Musa answered. "They're too far away. You might just be seeing what you want to see."

"If those are electric poles, that means there are people nearby. We have to go toward them!"

We didn't know if they were a hallucination produced by sheer force of will, but to us, they looked like power lines along a road. It was possible that we were finally approaching civilization, and as we got closer, our enthusiasm grew. Within a few hours, we could see that they were unmistakably power lines. We were elated, though our extreme exhaustion prevented us from jumping for joy. In fact, I didn't even manage to reach the village on my own two feet: I passed out before we got there. The last thing I remember was opening my mouth to cry out for help—to tell the others that I wasn't going to make it—but no words coming out.

The next thing I remember is water being poured over my head, trickling down my body, soaking me. It wasn't a dream; it was real. My five companions had carried me the rest of the way, saving my life.

Of the forty-six of us who had been abandoned in the desert, only six reached the village. The other forty had died in the sands of the Sahara. It was heartbreaking, excruciating. We cried our hearts out. We had traveled along the path through hell for three weeks.

LIBYA

We had succeeded in crossing the desert, even though only six of us had made it. I woke up in a tiny, arid village called Isir, not much more than a few houses in the sand. I was already on the other side of the Libyan border. The people there looked at us like we were tigers, or some kind of wild animal, and they ran from us, afraid. We had escaped from the desert's clutches. Even though we had miraculously managed to save our own lives, the fight to survive wasn't over.

When I woke in Isir, I could see a group of kids approaching us from a distance. As we walked toward the edge of the village, the women we passed ran away and locked themselves in their homes. At the time, we thought this was strange, because we didn't know that in Libya, women aren't allowed to speak to men other than their husbands. It was midday, and the sun was oppressive, so we took shelter under the roofs of a few shacks, which made a nice, shady spot. The children arrived and offered to sell us water—not the warm water Musa had used to revive me, but cold water from their refrigerators.

We had no money left. All I had was my empty wallet, which I traded to the children in exchange for that wonderful cold drink. We felt the cool liquid going down our throats and refreshing our bodies. One of the saddest things I learned on my journey is that in this life, no one gives you anything for free. They always want something in exchange: it's human nature. Or at least, it's the nature of the system that humans live in. If I hadn't been able to trade my wallet, even though it was hot in the desert and I was close to death, those children probably wouldn't have given me the water. I wasn't asking for a car, I wasn't asking for treasure—just water, because I had been walking through the Sahara for weeks. But that's how the world works.

We tried to tell the children that there were other migrants still in the desert. We pointed in the direction we'd come from, but we couldn't make them understand. Finally, some men arrived who spoke Hausa.

"We've just crossed the desert—we've been walking for three weeks," we said. "Our friends are still out there. They might still be alive, but we have to hurry!"

"We'll go take a look," said the man who seemed to be their leader, "but the desert is vast and treacherous. You think you see things where there are none; objects that appear close can be far away."

Several men got in a car and searched where we told them. They drove around and around, but didn't find anyone. There was no trace of the rest of our group. They almost certainly became another set of bodies in the mass grave of the desert.

Our hosts offered us milk to drink and dinner to eat: spaghetti with tomato sauce. In exchange, we helped repair some walls the next day. Shinonee, a member of our group, had some experience with brickwork. Three of our companions decided to leave the village the next day, but Shinonee, Musa, and I decided to stay for a week. The idea was to work for the people in Isir, earn some money, and continue to the next village. This proved to be complicated, though, since we were paid only in food.

My goal was to continue north until I reached Tripoli, the capital of Libya, on the Mediterranean coast. There, I would find a job that paid the monthly salary I'd been dreaming of. After a week in the village, Musa, Shinonee, and I resumed our journey on foot. Our next stop was Baragat, where we found work picking watermelons. Then we took a taxi to Ghat, in the southwest of the country, near the Algerian border. There was a Black enclave there—a space where migrants from sub-Saharan Africa lived in a shifting, ad hoc community—but it cost money to spend the night, and since we didn't have any money, we slept on cardboard on the street, even on windy nights. We spent a few weeks in Ghat, but work was hard to find, and we ended up drifting, living on the street, and asking restaurants for leftover scraps. It was very different from the life I'd hoped to find in Libya.

Eventually, a construction company hired us to dig seven-meter holes in the ground so they could place pillars for the foundation of a house. They paid five dinars per day, which, back then, was about one US dollar. The work was hard, and a nonimmigrant would have been paid more, but it beat begging on the street and never reaching Tripoli. For the most part, that was how we made it to the capital: we'd walk to the next village, work odd jobs, earn a little money, beg for food, and then do it all again. We passed through a long series of Libyan towns that way before we reached our destination, always worried someone would try to rob us. We met many other migrants making the same journey. Everyone's first priority was finding their next meal; arriving at the capital was a distant second.

With every passing day, my skin grew a little thicker. On one hand, I knew I could die, but on the other hand, I had nothing left to lose except my life. Despite all the hardship, I didn't regret making the journey. I never once considered going home, never felt nostalgic, never felt homesick. On that path, there is no turning back. You either make it alive or you die trying.

In fact, you couldn't go back if you wanted to. They say some people give up and go home, but I never met anyone who tried that. The smuggler networks don't even operate in that direction. I did meet plenty of sinkers, though, like the men I'd seen in Agadez: people who run out of money, can't find

North to Paradise

a way to earn more, and end up stuck halfway through their journey. Trapped for life.

—m—

As we walked on the road to Tripoli, somewhere between Ghat and Alawenat, I got a terrible nosebleed. It wouldn't stop, so we left the main road to ask for help at a military outpost we saw in the distance.

"We can't touch a Black man's blood," they told us when we arrived. "For us, that would be like touching a dog's blood. We can't help you."

Some Muslims won't touch dogs, because they're considered impure. Libya is in North Africa, and most people who live there aren't Black, they're Arab.

"Here, take these rags. That's all we can do for you." This exchange has been permanently etched in my memory.

That was the first time I understood that there is a thing called "racism." When I was in Ghana, in Black Africa, there was no racial discrimination. As I traveled farther in the world, I began to notice it. Of course, sometimes trucks hauling watermelons would pass us walking on the road, and the drivers would throw a few off for us. The fruit shattered on the asphalt, but we always devoured it anyway. My point is, we encountered plenty of good and generous people too.

In Ubari, a fairly large oasis town and the capital of the Wadi al Hayaa District in central Libya, we slept in an old shopping center that had been built for Americans working in the oil sector, then abandoned once they left. We lived there with others we'd met on our journey. Ubari was a tough place where you couldn't find work doing anything except harvesting melons. We woke at five in the morning and waited at a traffic circle in a specific part of town. Whenever anyone needed a laborer, they drove by and we raced to jump into their pickup truck. We had to outrun the other migrants looking for work, and competition was fierce. I was pretty quick, but even when I made it onto the truck, they almost never let me work:

"You're just a little kid—you're too young to pick melons! Get out of here!" Sometimes being young worked in my favor, but other times, it got in the way.

I was in Ubari for a long time. Since I rarely got work, I didn't have enough money to continue my journey. Musa and Shinonee were more successful. Once they had enough money, we agreed that they would wait for me in Sabha, a city that was three hours away by taxi. They didn't want to leave me alone, but I told them to go because when I finally made it to Sabha, they would already have a feel for the city and help me fit in. Still, I felt incredibly lonely and vulnerable in Ubari all by myself—I was still just a kid, alone in an unfamiliar place, unable to speak the language. But on the journey north, you adapt to sadness just like you adapt to everything else.

Being alone motivated me to try harder to find work. Eventually, an elderly man from the mosque hired me to build a fence around his garden. My first day on the job, after working for hours, the man came to find me. He gestured to his mouth, seeming to ask me if I'd had anything to eat. But of course, I hadn't—where would I have gotten food?

It turns out that he had asked a woman in his family to leave lunch for me outside the door. It may have been his daughter or his wife—I never knew, because I only ever saw her from a distance, and she covered her entire body except for her eyes. The prohibition on interactions between men and women meant she couldn't hand the food to me, and the language barrier meant the elderly man couldn't explain that they were going to feed me. So I'd gone hungry all afternoon, even though they had prepared a meal especially for me! He was a kind man, and I was grateful to him.

But not everyone was kind. One day, I met a man as we were both leaving the mosque after prayer.

"Are you hungry? Are you alone?" he asked.

"Of course I'm hungry."

"Well, come with me. Come to my house, I'll feed you, don't worry."

He said he would cook me dinner if I did the dishes. But almost as soon as we'd stepped through the door, he pushed me into a corner. He stripped off my clothes and tried to rape me, but I fought free, grabbed my shirt and pants, and ran out of the house. I cut myself jumping over a wall covered in broken glass—I still have the scar—but I had to get away from him. When I finally made it to the street, I was wearing only underwear. My first thought was that in Libya, I absolutely could not be undressed like that in public, so I hurried to dress before anyone saw.

After that, I was terrified all the time. If I wasn't safe even with someone I met at the mosque, then I wasn't safe anywhere. I tried to keep out of sight as much as possible. I was constantly looking over my shoulder, afraid that this man or someone else would attack me. Eventually, I earned enough money building the fence and doing other odd jobs that I could continue on to Sabha.

—⟋⟍—

Sabha is another key city on migration routes, where vast numbers of migrants from Nigeria, Niger, and Ghana converge on their journey north. There, I found work fixing trucks at an auto repair shop, and I stayed for two months to save money. Shinonee left shortly after I arrived, and that was the last time I saw him. A little later, Musa left: he had enough money to continue and hadn't found stable work like I had. We had become so close that it was hard to say goodbye, but after everything we had been through, grappling with difficult emotions was nothing new. We parted with a hug, unsure if we'd ever see each other again.

"We'll be all right. I know it," Musa assured me, ever the optimist.

"I'll see you in the Land of the Whites," I answered.

As I always did when I was alone in an unfamiliar place, I set out to make contact with an older person I could trust, someone who could help and protect me. I found a man who had been in Libya for eight years: at one point, he had lived in Tripoli, but the police gave him trouble there, so he had fled the coast. Now he was trying to go back. He said that if I paid for part of his bus ticket to Tripoli, he'd let me stay in his house there. Once again, I walked right into the trap: the house didn't exist. On the journey north, people are constantly trying to cheat you. Everyone's trying to survive, even at someone else's expense. The silver lining was that this man had lots of acquaintances in the city, and they directed us to a house in a remote part of the city where we could stay. We took a taxi.

It was what they call a "connection house," a sordid space used for sex trafficking and the sale of alcohol and marijuana. In short, a den of vice. Even though it looked like a regular building from the outside, it had a strange layout on the inside. The house was built around a large internal courtyard with a sand floor, where customers drank, smoked, and listened to music. It was like a bar. Several hallways led to small bedrooms where trafficked women were forced to work. My first days there, I swapped stories with the other new arrivals. We had a lot of experiences in common, and I felt less alone when I was among others who understood my struggles and aspirations. All of them talked about Europe like it was the best place in the world, the answer to all their problems, even though there was no evidence that this was true. But we believed what we wanted to believe and kept on hoping. We didn't even know that immigration is considered a problem in Europe. We were under the naïve impression that we would be welcomed with open arms. Lots of the other migrants in the connection house had family in Europe, and they were in Tripoli, waiting for someone to send them money. But of course the money never arrived.

The women forced to work in the connection house came from all over the continent, although the majority were from Nigeria. Almost all of them had been tricked: husbands or smugglers lead them north, promising to bring them to Paradise, but as soon as they set foot in Libya, these women essentially become human merchandise. The men who smuggle them into the country act as their pimps, and they're bought and sold in connection houses throughout the country. It was hard for male immigrants like me to earn enough money to survive, but at least we could look for voluntary work. With the extreme gender discrimination in Libya, these women couldn't find jobs and had no choice but to work for the men who tricked them. It's a miserable, dishonest system, and a horrible form of exploitation.

Alcohol is illegal and hard to find in Libya, so they distilled it in the connection house over an open flame, using complex apparatuses wrapped in tubes. I don't know what kind of alcohol it was, but it must have been very low quality, and extremely potent. They stored it in large metal tins and drank it from shot glasses. Alcohol is the most potent drug in Libya, but you never see anyone walking around drunk or making a spectacle of himself, which could attract the attention of the police, who would take you to prison. That was too high a price to pay, so they drank and left. People almost never brought alcohol back to their homes. Even the smell could give you away, so before leaving, customers would eat roasted corn to cover their breath. It was a risky business. In a different part of the house, there was another, tidier room with a cement floor, which was used for smoking hashish and marijuana.

The clientele consisted mostly of Takums. *Takum* is a slang word used among migrants in Libya. It's not Arabic or English or Hausa or any other language; it's part of the unique jargon that forms when you have people from so many different parts of the world come together in one place. It means someone who belongs to Libya's class of somewhat well-established Black people, migrants who have been in the country for a few years. The opposite of a Takum is an abba fresh, a Black migrant who only recently arrived, with no money and no connections. I was an abba fresh.

Takums come to Libya from all over sub-Saharan Africa, from countries like Ghana and Nigeria and Chad, where alcohol is legal and relations between men and women are much more open. They aren't used to Libya's strict sexual prohibitions, so many of them turn to the services provided through the connection houses' system of exploitation. This isn't true of all Takums, of course, and there were some customers who came for the alcohol and marijuana but not the women. There were also some Arab Muslims who came to the connection house, trying to skirt religious prohibitions.

My first night, I slept in the bedroom where Akosua—a young, beautiful Ghanaian girl from the Ashanti tribe who had been forced into prostitution—worked during the day; no space was ever left unused in that place. She couldn't have been older than seventeen. We didn't talk at first: we were both scared and vulnerable. But one night, when I got back to the house at one or two in the morning, she started a conversation:

"Are you okay? You look sick." I hadn't expected her to say anything, and I was taken off guard.

"I couldn't find any work today, or yesterday. I haven't been able to eat."

"Here, take some bread." I had felt so sorry for her, and here she was helping me.

On my journey north, I saw so many people behaving worse than animals, motivated by such greed that they had no humanity. But then a person who was more vulnerable and exploited than I was reached out and shared what little she had. These are the moments that I try to remember, moments of our shared humanity.

Akosua and I started talking, and for a short time, we were friends. She told me that she never expected to end up in a place like that, forced to sell her body. Her boyfriend had promised to take her to the Land of the Whites. To pay for their passage to Libya, he'd borrowed money from smugglers affiliated with the connection house, and when they reached Tripoli, her boyfriend sold her to the pimps. Now she had to sell her body to pay off his debt, but the amount she owed seemed to just keep growing. Her only dream was to get out of there, to be free. I told her about how most of my companions died crossing the Hoggar Mountains, and she told me about her own trip across the Sahara, by a different route. I felt helpless because there was nothing I could do for her: I had no authority in that place, no money to give her. All I could do was listen and offer my sympathy. The connection house was a heart-wrenching, horrible place, especially for a devout young Muslim like me, who prayed every day. You could get anything in that connection house. The only thing you couldn't find was God.

When I was "on call," I had to do miscellaneous tasks to earn my keep, like hand out the small doses of marijuana they sold or make a note on the wall every time one of the women performed a service. That way, when the pimps came at night, they knew how many customers had come through and made sure the trafficked women were paying up. They kept the girls in a state of strict subjugation, so as not to miss a single cent. The house must have been owned by a Libyan because it's almost impossible for a migrant to own a house in Libya, even if you're a Takum. I never knew who was really in charge. I just knew that whenever someone gave me an order, I did what he said. I spent as much time outside of the house as possible: I woke up before sunrise, went to look for work, and didn't return until midnight at the earliest. This was partly to increase my odds of finding work, but also because there were always pimps, smugglers, and gang members around, and I wanted to be away as much as possible.

—⁓—

After three nights in the house, the man whose bus ticket I had paid for brought me to another one. Some Ghanaian men were trying to build their own connection house from scratch, creating their own business. Since they were from our country, we went with them. As a cover for the illegal operation, some of us stood outside, acting like we were doing construction work on the building, while others kept watch.

There was an elderly woman in that house, who was also working for the pimps. I don't know how long she had been forced to work that way. She mocked me whenever I started praying: "Don't waste your time," she'd snap. "Your God doesn't listen to prayers from a place like this." I had seen a lot of suffering by that point, and I had experienced a lot of suffering myself, but I still prayed five times a day, and I still believed in God. My faith was what had made so many parts of this journey bearable.

One miraculous day, I was sent to fetch water at a nearby fountain. I grabbed a couple of empty jugs and headed out. As I was lugging the water back to the house, I was shocked to see it surrounded by police cars. They had discovered what it was being used for. I dropped the jugs and ran as fast as I could in the opposite direction. I was unspeakably lucky to be out of the house at that particular moment. Otherwise, I would have ended up in a Libyan prison, probably one of the most wretched places in the world. In Libya, there is no concept of human rights. If they catch you, you die in prison. I ran all the way to downtown Tripoli, and with the little money I had, I bought a ticket to Benghazi, the second-biggest city in the country, in the northwest, also on the Mediterranean coast.

After all my hopes and efforts to get there, I had only been in Tripoli for a week.

After just one week in Tripoli, I spent four years in Benghazi; that's how unpredictable the journey north can be. Sometimes you leave a place when you've only just arrived, you're just a blip, as if you were never even there. Other times, you end up waiting for what seems like an eternity, and you build something resembling a life. Nothing is certain.

The cities along my journey seemed to keep getting bigger and more wondrous. Benghazi was beautiful, with tall buildings and expansively open public spaces. It looked like a European metropolis, and it even made Accra, Ghana's capital city, look small by comparison. There had been a lot of bloody battles there during the Libyan civil wars, when it was a rebel bastion against Muammar al-Qaddafi. The city is strongly associated with anti-Qaddafi sentiment, but he ruled with such an iron fist that the people there would hesitate to speak critically of him out loud, even if there was no one else around. If you were caught publicly criticizing his leadership, you would disappear overnight.

When I arrived, I went to a restaurant to beg for scraps. By sheer dumb luck, the woman managing the restaurant was Wala, a member of my tribe. She fed me and paid for a taxi to take me to an all-Black tenement in the Al Kish neighborhood. She told me not to knock on the door: instead I should throw a stone at the building in a specific way so they would let me in. It was a kind of password, meant to keep out suspicious strangers. Since over fifty people often lived in the same house, it was hard to keep track of who was who.

The tenement was a dilapidated, unpainted brick building in the ghetto. There were no windows, just holes in the wall covered with rags. I had no trouble getting in; no one asked me any questions. As the sun set, I listened to their conversations in Ashanti, which is the second-most-common language in Ghana after English. One man seemed to be in charge: he was big, with a white beard, white hair, and no shirt, displaying his semispherical belly proudly. Eventually, he noticed me.

"I don't recognize your face. Who are you?" he asked.

"My name is Ousman. I just got here."

"Are you stupid or something? Why didn't you say anything?" he asked. "You were silent this whole time, and now it's late. Everyone's going to bed, and we don't know where you'll sleep. Where are we going to fit you in?" It was a logistical problem. Though he commanded respect, he seemed like a kind man.

"Who did you travel with?"

"Nobody. I left from Accra on my own and crossed the Sahara on foot. I've been working my way across Libya—I only just left Tripoli."

"Well!" he exclaimed. "Seems like you're quite the traveler. Even more adventurous than me!"

He was surprised because most migrants travel in groups, or at least with one other person. A companion you can confide in, someone you trust entirely who will support you in times of crisis.

In the tenement, people slept in groups in the many bedrooms, but there were only two or three bathrooms, fouler than anything you can imagine. They were exceedingly disgusting; I'm still amazed that more people don't get sick in those places. The night I arrived, there was no space in any of the bedrooms, so the man in charge asked where I was from so he could place me with my compatriots. He ended up putting me in a room with other Ghanaians from Brong-Ahafo, my region of the country, which generates lots of immigration.

"Hey!" he yelled into a room. "We've got one of yours here! Make space!"

There were five guys from Techiman sleeping there.

"There's no room!" a voice called out.

They didn't want to let me sleep there at first, but eventually, they gave in. I had to pay five dinars per week—around four US dollars. At one point, seven of us lived in that room, sleeping on the floor covered wall to wall in mattresses.

There was a spirit of camaraderie in the tenement. We cooked our meals in a corner on a gas camping stove. For dishes, we had some mugs, a few empty tomato tins, and a couple of plates. Our most frequent recipe involved making a sauce from old, nearly rotten tomatoes that Libyans had thrown away and mixing it with tuna and salt. Occasionally, we cooked rice in a pot and added it to our sauce, or we'd mix a bit of flour with water to make a kind of dough to dip in the sauce. We'd chop tomatoes and onions and eat them with bread, like a kind of salad. That was pretty much all we had to eat. Sometimes, there was bread and canned sardines, or the occasional piece of fruit. We had no idea how much variety of food there is in the world. When we fantasized about getting a proper meal, we'd just imagine kilos and kilos of rice with tomato and tuna. When Libyans in the neighborhood got married, we'd pick up the scraps after the wedding was over, and sometimes, after Friday prayers, the locals would cook extra food and offer it to us. Even though we encountered a lot of cruelty, there are kind and caring people wherever you go.

At night, we'd sit in the hallway and talk. Everyone had their own story to tell, and I got a lot of respect because I'd followed the route from Agadez across the desert and over the Hoggar Mountains, which are famously treacherous. Few people had taken my route, and fewer survived.

"You had some rotten luck, Ousman," they told me. "That's the hard way to go."

The other route, by truck through Duruku, was much simpler, though it had its own challenges. Sometimes, migrants get ambushed and assaulted by robbers. Trucks overburdened with migrants break down. Many others in the tenement had also been abandoned in the middle of the desert. It broke my heart to talk to a Banda man in my room named Cadre: he'd given up everything to emigrate, and regretted it. He had sold his two taxis and his shop, which had provided him a decent life back home. But he had been bewitched, enchanted by the prospect of traveling to the Land of the Whites. He cried almost every night.

There were different social classes in the tenement. For example, there was a man from Techiman named Adeibi who had a stable job with a construction company that contracted with the University of Benghazi. He earned decent money, as much as fifty US dollars a month. For us, that was a lot. In Ghana, he had been a truck mechanic.

"The university girls always say hello to me in English when they see me. When no one's looking, they sneak past and go, 'Hi, Adeibi!'"

But the girl he lost sleep over was a poor, young Ghanaian.

"If I make it to Europe and get rich, I'll go back to Ghana to give her a real future."

From his elegant clothes, you could tell he earned a better living than most of us. On Sundays, he'd put on khaki pants and a white shirt, plus jewelry and other accessories. He really liked getting dressed up. Clothes were a way of signaling status. He wasn't a novice like me; he'd been in Libya for a while, and he'd figured out a few things. The wealthier migrants had other luxuries too: instead of sleeping seven to a bedroom, they usually had only two roommates. In places like that, it's normal to have a protector. I always tried to cultivate friendships with people who could help and protect me, so I would often fold Adeibi's clothes or do his dishes. I slowly won him over. People laughed and said that Adeibi was my boss, but I didn't mind. He would give me food, and we became good friends.

Soon I found work in a body repair shop in the Bodema District. They had me repair a badly damaged Hyundai Pony for free to prove my skills. When they saw the results, they hired me, and I worked there for six months, sharing a bunk above the workshop with a boy named Ali.

Eventually, we had a problem. The workshop was owned by a Palestinian man named Mohammed who didn't know how to do the work himself, which is why he hired me to do the metalwork and Ali to do the painting. He dealt with the customers, and we were supposed to divide the profits between the three of us. But one day, we discovered Mohammed was charging the customers more than he told us and pocketing the difference—he was cheating us. Ali called him a liar. In Islam, that's the worst accusation you can make; it's worse than punching someone. Mohammed became enraged and started shouting. We thought he might kill us, so we ran away. I returned to the tenement.

I managed to establish myself in Benghazi, working here and there, coming and going between different workshops. My everyday life was as normal as it could be in Libya. I never got used to the ways men and women interacted there, which was governed by strict rules. Taxis and buses are segregated by gender: you aren't allowed to get into a vehicle with a woman, and if you find yourself near a woman on the sidewalk, you have to cross the street. Or at least, you do if you're Black. You also never see a woman alone outside: she's always with her father, her husband, or an older brother. And of course, you wouldn't even dream of looking at a woman. If the man she's with catches you, he'll start throwing rocks.

One of the biggest problems in the city were the violent street gangs of young Libyan men called "the Asma Boys." Instead of wearing traditional clothing, they dressed like westerners: sneakers, cuffed jeans, etc. If they saw a Black man on the street, they would beat him until he couldn't breathe. We had to be very careful to avoid them, and tried to stay in populated areas. They hated Black people because in 2000, after traveling across Africa, Muammar al-Qaddafi had decided to reduce funding for Libyan social programs because that kind of support didn't exist elsewhere on the continent. The Asma Boys blamed us, and that's where their hatred came from. Once, when I was walking with my friend Mustafa, they jumped us and left Mustafa badly injured. I managed to get away. Sometimes they kidnap Black people for ransom. Other times, they just kill us.

There is almost no concept of leisure or recreation in Libya. There are no movie theaters. There are only three TV channels, and they mostly play footage of Qaddafi railing against the United States. In our rare moments of free time, we watched DVDs in some Takum's house. On Fridays after work, we would get together to watch music videos. We had seen so little Western media, and sexuality was so thoroughly repressed in Libya, that Shakira's videos seemed almost illicit. We'd never seen women like that, in so little clothing, moving so seductively. A favorite was "Whenever, Wherever," where Shakira crawls in the mud and dances with the waves crashing all around her, shaking her hips sensually. We also liked Jennifer Lopez and some rappers from the US, like 50 Cent. I wonder if these music superstars know that people as poor as we were, in such precarious circumstances, watch their videos. Do they know their music reaches these places and these people? For us, those days were like a holiday. The rest of the week was monotonous, endless work.

—∞—

In Benghazi, I was reunited with my friend Musa. In every city, there's a place where Black people gather to share our experiences and exchange information, and if you're Black, it's easy to find. In Benghazi, it was in the Al Funduq neighborhood. One day, someone there mentioned a boy named Musa from Kumasi who was working in town. I managed to find him.

We were so happy to be together again. Imagine being alone in the middle of the wilderness, with no other humans for miles around. That was how I felt in that city, with no family, friends, or connections. Being reunited by chance with my best friend brought the greatest feeling of relief in the world. On such a lonely and painful journey, Musa was my only lifeline. He was so much more than a friend: he was like my father, and like a brother, and a sister, and a mother, all wrapped into one. He was everything to me. In all of Benghazi, in all of Libya, we found each other; the odds of us being there at the same time were so low that it felt like divine intervention.

He had found a night job working as a security guard, so he slept during the day, but it wasn't a very demanding job: he just walked around the premises every once in a while. He didn't live in the Black tenement, but in a large shipping container—the kind you see on boats—which had been adapted as a bedroom. It was a pretty cool place, and I loved spending the night there. I would usually visit on Thursdays, and we'd stay up the entire night, talking about soccer and American singers. It was the happiest part of my week. He knew all about music because he had a ton of CDs, whereas I knew almost nothing. He also had plenty of food, kilos of rice and tuna and tomatoes, and even soda. We ate as much as we wanted. Musa was always tired because he had a hard time sleeping when the sun was up. Musa's shipping container was my favorite place to be; it felt like my home. I was always sad on Friday mornings when I had to go back to the workshop, which I hated.

Sometimes, on Fridays, we would go to the governor of Benghazi's house because Musa's cousin Mohammed was the "house boy," the servant in charge of making coffee and doing other small tasks. It was an enormous, luxurious home. Mohammed lived in a small house that was just for him, and it was unbelievably luxurious too; he even had his own kitchen and bathroom. The governor had been an ally of Qaddafi when he came to power, and in his garage, he had a collection of fifty cars. One of Mohammed's jobs was to start each car at regular intervals so the batteries wouldn't die.

Around three years after our reunion, Musa decided he had to continue onward. He was finally ready to cross into Europe, by way of Casablanca. I was more cautious: my plan was to save as much money as possible. We said goodbye again, certain that we'd be reunited in the Land of the Whites.

I got a job at the port, working for a Lebanese man named Adel, where I welded the oil extraction tubes and other miscellaneous parts for heavy-duty vehicles (excavators and machines like that). It was a huge workshop at the outskirts of town near the airport, guarded by ten dogs. Everywhere I went, there were hardworking Palestinians, Lebanese . . . but the Libyans didn't work much. They got money just for having children. The more kids they had, the more money they received, because there are only five million of them occupying an enormous territory, and they have a massive amount of oil. So they were paid just for being Libyan. They are very rich people: the government has empty apartments that it makes available to anyone who wants to live there, but in Libya, they think only poor people live in apartments: everyone is expected to have a house of their own. Meanwhile, we Black folks lived differently, on the outskirts, in the slums.

———ɯɯ———

Many of the migrants you see on the news, arriving on the Mediterranean coast or dying at sea, depart from Libya. There, smugglers cram them onto rubber or wooden rafts and shove them out to sea. Sometimes they pack as many as four hundred people onto a single raft. I knew people who tried to cross there, where smugglers charge a thousand dollars for passage to Europe. Often these people came back, saying they had been cheated out of their money.

When I was in Ghana, I thought the Land of the Whites lay just across the sea. I thought the same thing in Libya, but from Tripoli, it was actually true. Italy, Greece, and Malta aren't far from the Libyan coast. My plan was to save as much money as possible before taking the leap, and as my savings grew, I began to consider the best way to cross. Everyone talked about leaving from Zuwarah, a coastal town near Tripoli. They said it was the easiest way—just a short raft trip across the Mediterranean, from the Libyan coast to Europe. It sounded easy. Some people got very excited at the prospect: they wanted to get to the north as quickly as possible. But I knew it was best to keep calm. I'm a pretty patient person, and I didn't want to end up penniless halfway down the road. I wanted to make sure I had a good shot before I took it. What I didn't know was that many twists and turns still lay ahead.

You usually get paid in dinars in Libya, and when you have a hundred saved up, you exchange them for US dollars. But I knew it was best not to hurry. I kept track of the exchange rate between the dollar and the dinar and waited for the best moment to cash out. At one point, I had over one thousand dinars saved. I didn't want to carry that much money on me, but I couldn't leave it where I slept either (in case someone tried to steal it), so I buried it somewhere secret, like a treasure. In fact, it was all the treasure I had.

Four years later, I had enough money saved. For better or for worse, it was time to go. I had to take the leap.

—m—

I had never been on an airplane, but I had to get to Tripoli in order to continue my journey, and at that time, Qaddafi was visiting his hometown of Sirte—between Tripoli and Benghazi—so the highway was full of checkpoints. If you're Black and stopped at a checkpoint in Libya, you're in trouble. At any moment, for no reason, they might put you in jail, where you will rot until the end of your days.

So I decided I would fly for the first time in my life. I bought a Ghanaian passport on the black market, glued in my own photo, and went to the airport. There are several different kinds of police in Libya. They say that the cops with the red berets are accountable to no one, they can kill you on the spot. When Qaddafi is in town, they are the ones who protect him. In the airport, at the time, there were three checkpoints. At all three, the police looked at my passport, then at my face, then back at my passport. My knees were shaking, but they let me through. It was my lucky day; if they'd caught me, I might still be in a prison right now.

The airplane was enormous, but my fear was even bigger. We took our place on the runway, then accelerated, faster and faster and faster—I could feel my face being forced backward until the colossal metal machine rose from the ground as if by magic. At last I was on one of those airplanes I had seen gliding across the sky from my village, one of those contraptions I had found so fascinating. How does something that heavy stay in the sky? During takeoff, I felt sick to my stomach when I saw that the front of the plane was tilting upward and pulling off the earth, and even sicker as everything below us grew smaller and smaller. I clutched the armrest for the entire flight, as if I could prevent the plane from falling back to the ground.

This time, I arrived in Tripoli well dressed and with money in my pockets. It was very different from my first visit to the city, when I was wearing torn clothing after my tortuous journey through the desert and across the country, going from village to village.

The capital is where things happen. I went to eat in the city's Black enclave. This time, I knew where to go for information and where all the important places were. I went to the slums, where you can learn anything you want to know and get your hands on anything you need. The slums are almost a means of communication in and of themselves, an alternative radio station, a social network, because everybody passes through there, and everybody talks. In that hodgepodge of people, there are also guides eager to find migrants whom they can introduce to the smugglers who organize trips north.

"I've got contacts. I know people who can help you cross," one of them said. "You should come with me. They're serious people, your safest option."

He seemed trustworthy. I hired him for one hundred dollars.

TUNISIA, ALGERIA, MALI, MOROCCO, MAURITANIA

We took the bus from Tripoli to Ghadames, the town from which several other migrants and I would cross the border into Tunisia on foot. We would leave at midnight and walk until we reached the first Tunisian village, where a smuggler would pick us up. I carried so much water that I could barely move; I wasn't making the same mistake as the last time I went into the desert, though this trek was much shorter. We hiked all night until we reached that first village, where several Land Rovers were waiting for us. They picked us up, brought us to another house, and the whole cycle started again.

When I talk about smugglers like this, it's not what you're imagining. Europeans always picture hardened criminals with AK-47s like in the movies, but that's not the case. They're just people with connections, and together they make up a vast, loose network that shuttles migrants north. They don't trick or pressure anyone into traveling to Europe; they're simply responding to a demand. In Ghana, no one brainwashed me into beginning my journey; I was driven by my own eagerness to see the world. It's true, though, that these organizations can acquire whatever documents you need, like a false passport. The different criminal organizations form a chain, and you work your way from one link to the next along your journey. It's all connected.

The Land Rovers crossed the desert at breakneck speeds. Our drivers were very skilled; they could have won the Dakar Rally. They knew the desert well and were clearly very experienced. Climbing a dune, the driver had the gas pedal on the floor, and as we reached the crest, he managed to maintain control of the vehicle even when it felt like we were flying, suspended in the air, before landing hard back on the ground. It was like they were steering a speedboat, catching air above the waves, rather than driving a car over sand dunes. Some passengers nearly vomited. We traveled like that for days, crossing the desert in stages.

Just before reaching Ouargla in Algeria, we ran out of water. We decided to get out of our vehicles and search for a well at solar noon, when the sun is at its hottest and there are fewer patrols out, since that's when the police usually take their break. But before long, we heard gunshots. Police were approaching in a car, firing their weapons in the air and screaming like madmen. We panicked. Around ten of us jumped back into the cars and sped away. The police could chase only one vehicle, and unfortunately, it was the Land Rover I was in. They shot at us, trying to blow out our tires. A few passengers clinging to the outside of the car were hit. The other Land Rovers managed to escape, but we were intercepted, along with the migrants who hadn't been able to get back in the car.

The police grabbed our driver and threw him on the ground, mercilessly striking him on the head over and over with the butts of their rifles. They literally broke his face open, and kept beating him until it was mangled and covered in blood.

"Why didn't you stop, huh? Why didn't you stop?" they demanded as they beat him. "Imbecile, we ordered you to stop!"

They nearly killed him. They were the worst cops I've ever encountered in my life. Horrible, and violent.

There were seven of us in the vehicle, and around seven others who hadn't made it back into the Land Rovers. The police called for backup to transport us to a control center, where they counted us over and over again. After that, they took us to a police station, and then on a strange tour of different holding centers: we went from one foul, unsanitary prison to another. In each place, they took down our information; there was a lot of paperwork everywhere. They put us in a prison in Tamanrasset, in the heart of the desert. Algeria receives economic support from France to stop migration, so in each prison, they gave us a different name. That way, they could claim they were detaining many more immigrants than they really were, and get more money. If it weren't for that, I assume they would have brought us straight to our destination.

In Samasasud, we stayed in the prison for two days. They packed us seven to a cell, and I was very sick with a fever. There was a smuggler from Techiman with us who had a lot of money from sneaking marijuana across the Moroccan border. He kept the cash in his underwear so the Arab guards couldn't find it; they never search that area of your body. As a smuggler, he had been arrested in Algeria many times, so he knew they would keep transferring us from prison to prison in order to make more money, even though legally we should have been deported. He decided we should try to make ourselves more trouble than we were worth, so he goaded a very surly, very dumb prisoner named Kofi into inciting a riot: Kofi started screaming that he wanted to be let out, and soon several other inmates joined in. They were sick of being treated like merchandise, and they clamored to be released, lashing out at the guards.

The police called for reinforcements, who arrived with large batons and beat all of us like animals. They were unrelentingly cruel; if you're a Black man in an Algerian prison, you have no rights whatsoever. I received one very hard blow to the head, and when I fell to the ground, they continued to beat me until they realized I might die. Even though I was still conscious, I was in a horrible state, bleeding, in pain, with bruises all over my body. They called an ambulance to pick me up, handcuffed me, brought me to the hospital, and hooked me up to some kind of machine. I'm still not sure what procedures they performed on me. Eventually, I opened my eyes. A policeman named Mohamed was sitting beside me. I immediately had a good feeling about him. He asked what my name was, took an interest in my health, and chatted with me.

"You shouldn't get involved in this kind of trouble," he suggested.

"What happened?" I asked.

"You all made quite a stir in the prison, and of course, the guards had to do something about it. But don't worry, it'll turn out okay. If you ever find yourself back in Algeria, you've got a friend."

We formed a kind of temporary friendship while he was guarding me; it was one of the few moments of humanity that I encountered on my journey. My spirits were low: seemingly all of a sudden, I'd ended up in a bad situation, and I wondered if leaving my relatively stable and comfortable position in Benghazi had been the right decision.

When I was brought back to the cell, my fellow prisoners were all handcuffed. Kofi was crying when I returned, because he'd slept with his hands shackled behind his back and his whole arm was throbbing.

"I can't take the pain anymore," he cried out between sobs.

They continued to move us from prison to prison, all in the worst conditions imaginable, where we slept and ate only a few meters away from the always-overflowing toilet. Finally, they sent us to the border between Algeria and Mali, a no-man's-land. They told us to walk south, then drove off. They were kicking us out of the country, leaving us to try our luck in the middle of the desert. We walked until we found a few shacks, then waited. And of course, before long, some smugglers drove up and offered to take us back north to Tamanrasset, for a fee. They found a place for us to hide, then brought us to Ouargla, where we again headed north, retracing our steps. It was like they were playing hide-and-seek with the Algerian police.

—⁓m⁓—

In the no-man's-land between Algeria and Morocco, hidden from the world, lies the Valley, where the smuggler networks run a sort of autonomous state. They even have their own police. One of the smugglers, named Idrisu, had been arrested by the Algerian police with over fifty fake passports in his possession. He was tall, and so thin he looked ill: you could see each of his bones, and the corners of his mouth were always pale and dry. I had met him in the Tamanrasset prison, a horrific place where you had to constantly watch out for the guards because they would beat you for no reason at all. He was with me when we were released at the Algerian border, and the one who brought me to the smuggler city-state. In exchange, I paid for his bus ticket.

After being released by the Algerian police and making our way back to Ouargla, we met Abbas, known locally as "the President," a leading trafficker with a stash of over 150 passports from Mali, Burkina Faso, and other French-speaking countries. One by one, he grabbed a passport, held it up to see if we were a close enough match to the photo, and handed it to us.

I took the passport from him.

"What's your name?" he asked.

"Ousman."

He smacked me across the face. After a few seconds, he asked again:

"What's your name?"

"Ousman."

Another slap. Why? Why was he hitting me? Finally, I realized the way to make it stop was to say the name that appeared on the passport.

"What's your name?"

As soon as I responded with the correct name, he let me go. This was his way of making sure you never forgot your new identity. Some guys took a long time to figure it out.

With our new passports, six of us took a bus from Ouargla to the Valley. Not some kind of secret, clandestine bus—just a regular, commercial bus, with a few transfers. I knew the smuggler city-state would be one of my final stops before I departed for Paradise. I didn't know how, but I knew I would make it. We stopped at a small village just before the Valley. There, Idrisu said, "From here on out, we won't have any trouble. I've got it all taken care of."

There is no law in the Valley. As we approached on foot, we saw a camp and a checkpoint under a tree. There's a riverbed running through the Valley, but the river is dry, and the settlement stretches up the side of a hill beyond the riverbed. We identified ourselves. Idrisu had been telling the truth: he was a member of the organization, so they didn't give us any trouble.

We were taken to the leader of the camp, Razak, but everyone called him "the Tiger." His hut was made of cardboard and other scrap materials like all the other buildings in the Valley. But the smugglers' area was at the top of a hill, and cleaner than the rest. Razak's soldiers were unpleasant, but Razak himself was friendly enough. He greeted us, wearing nothing but his underwear:

"Welcome! Here, you are safe. We have a few rules: if you behave yourselves, nothing will happen to you. If you don't, the consequences will be severe."

Razak had recently taken power after leading a coup d'état in the Valley, during which several people had died. I was nervous around his bodyguard, who had a menacing look.

Migrants lived together, each in a different area. Razak was a Dagomba, and he lived at the top of the hill with his people. The Valley is also home to many sinkers, those who end up penniless halfway through their journey, with no way to continue onward and no way to go back home, like the men in Agadez. Some were stuck there forever, working for the smuggler networks.

Everyone is armed in the Valley; it's a place of life or death. Everyone there carried a machete, everyone was covered in cuts and scars, and everyone smoked marijuana, which was easy to get. It helped them get through the day. Even in such cruel environments, it's important to take time to clear your head. When I was there, there was a soccer match between Malians and Ghanaians (we won). At night, they gather and sing songs with beautiful melodies, but violent, tragic themes. Just like the word *Takum*, these songs aren't in any one language; they combine words from different cultures.

Mama no dey-oh (Mama isn't here)
Shiwa-lele shiwa-lele
Who go bail you? (Who will pay your bail?)
Shiwa-lele shiwa-lele
Make I no dey-oh (I wish I weren't here)
No go fiti ke-lele (But it's too late to escape)

Make I no die-oh (I don't want to die)
Who wan die? (Who wants to die?)

Na papa na giademan (Father is a guide)

Eh mama na ashawo (Mother is a prostitute)
Na piki go be baster (The baby will be a bastard)
Emo-emo-emo

Na mama polici-oh (Mother used to be a cop)
Na papa polici-eh (Father used to be a cop)
Na me I no dey-oh (But here I am)
Na today wahalah (Here I am today in this horrible situation)

N'Arab-oh people (The Arab people)
N'Arab-oh people wan carry me go (The Arab people want to arrest me)
Na Morocco people (The Moroccan people)
Na Morocco people wan carry me go (The Moroccan people want to arrest me)
Eh somebody go die (Somebody's going to die)
Eh-eh somebody go die (Somebody's going to die)

Ay logo logo logo (Let me have fun)
Ay logo logo logo dancing (Let me have fun dancing)
Ay logo logo logo (Let me have fun)
Ay logo logo logo dancing (Let me have fun dancing)

Who be giademan? (Who will be the guide?)
Who be passenger? (Who will be his passenger?)

When we reach Rabat we go know
(When we reach Rabat we will know)

Most people paid four hundred dollars to enter the Valley, but I was allowed in for free because I'd paid for Idrisu's bus ticket. Since I arrived with a trusted soldier, I was considered trustworthy too. I didn't even have to live in the same part of the camp as the other migrants: they placed me with the fifty or so people the smugglers hired to assist with operations. In the Valley, everyone sleeps in different areas based on their country of origin, and when it's time to leave, they use different channels. The Valley operates as a kind of migrant distribution center. They bring more and more people in until they reach a critical mass, and then a group crosses into Morocco.

When it was my turn to leave, they brought us to the capital city of Rabat under cover of night. Rabat looked like a European city to me—it was beautiful. In fact, I wondered if we had already arrived in the Land of the Whites. There, under a bridge, we met men with machetes who represented the three African smuggling kingpins: the three head smugglers who organize the clandestine ocean voyages to Europe on rafts, dinghies, and other small boats. Each kingpin offers his own way north, and each has his own network of soldiers. They're extremely powerful.

I decided to cross with Rajman's network—he's the most important smuggler of them all. I saw him only two or three times: he was an elegant, imposing man, no older than forty, who dressed in American clothes and looked like a hip-hop star, with gold chains and other jewelry. He had three houses in Morocco, his smuggling empire was firmly established, and he led a life of luxury. Even in the Valley, the three kingpins are already trying to persuade you, from a distance, to cross into Europe through their network—they send representatives to sell you on their routes. Rajman's emissaries, for example, were always talking up the "Rajman connection." Whoever does a better job marketing himself in the Valley ends up with more passengers when they arrive in Rabat, and each passenger pays a thousand dollars for a spot on a dinghy. It's a business like any other.

By this point, I had only six hundred dollars, so I had to ask for help from a distant cousin in Ghana who I'd seen only once before in my life. He owned the largest cassette store in the town of Wa, as well as a few other businesses: he was a successful entrepreneur. I told the smugglers that his shop was located by the only stoplight in the town, and that was enough for them to find him. They contacted him through a member of the Dagomba tribe, who share a border with the Wala, and the two peoples have established a kind of friendship through shared historical bonds. In Wa, their Dagomba messenger found my cousin and put him on the phone to speak to the smugglers.

"We've got your cousin Ousman here," they said, "and he needs four hundred dollars. We can torture and kill him, or you can give us four hundred dollars. Which will it be?"

To prove it, they put me on the phone.

"Please, give them the money or they'll kill me," I begged. "I don't have any other choice."

It was a significant amount of money for him, but he gave it to the smugglers' messenger, saving my life.

—⁓—

We weren't in Rabat long before they started sending us to Casablanca in groups of three. We traveled like normal passengers on commercial buses, not along a smuggler route. We cleaned up first, then boarded the buses with false passports. Even though we were traveling together, we acted like we didn't know each other, without chatting or sitting next to each other.

They picked us up in Casablanca and put us in a basement known as "Downblow," where passengers wait to be taken to the coast. There I met Sadic, Abbas's cousin. After a few minutes, I recognized another face—astonishingly, I was again reunited with Musa. I couldn't believe my luck. I thought we had said our final goodbye in Benghazi before he left for Casablanca, but he hadn't yet managed to get out of the city. When I saw him, I couldn't help thinking about when I was a kid learning the Qur'an in school. I'd been taught that all things are predestined, that all events that occur on Earth are part of God's plan. As my journey brought Musa and me together over and over again, against the wildest odds . . . All I can say is that it felt miraculous, like God intended for us to be together. And I was so thankful: in such terrifying circumstances, having a trustworthy friend can mean the difference between life and death, between becoming a sinker or reaching the next leg of your journey.

The powerful Rajman made one courtesy visit to Downblow, to make it clear that he was the one calling the shots. "Be grateful! Because you're with me, you'll arrive safe and sound," he told us pompously.

In that basement in Casablanca, we met several women who had been trafficked and subjected to unspeakable sexual violence. Many had become pregnant and were now traveling with newborn babies: children of the connection houses. Even with all the suffering I experienced, I know that my hardship pales in comparison to what female migrants endure. At least I had some freedom. But in a country like Libya, where women must be accompanied in public by a male family member, it's impossible for female migrants to find work, and they have no choice but to enter de facto slavery in the country's forced prostitution networks. Otherwise, they don't eat. Rape is so commonplace along the journey north, in and out of the connection houses, that these women have to find ways of coping with it; if they didn't somehow adapt to their reality—if they fully acknowledged and processed this violence—the trauma could kill them.

After a week in Downblow, they brought us to an unfurnished apartment. They warehoused us for several weeks there, during which time we never saw the sun. It was hard to even turn around when we slept, because we were packed like sardines. You couldn't walk to the bathroom without stepping on someone. The man in charge of the apartment slept more comfortably: he lived in a tent on the balcony that he had all to himself. We were there day and night, not allowed to leave under any circumstances, because we couldn't risk being seen. We couldn't even talk: we were reprimanded if our whispers got too loud, because a neighbor might hear us. One of the smugglers brought us provisions. One day, the gas canister we cooked with caught fire, and we had to open the door and throw it down the stairs. It fell enshrouded in flames. It's a small miracle no one called the Moroccan police.

From Casablanca, we set out for Mauritania, to the south. They told us that in Mauritania, we'd get on dinghies and set sail for Europe. We always traveled *hiki hiki*, which is what they call the practice of crossing borders in a zigzag pattern to minimize the chances of being intercepted. It had been three months since I left Libya.

—m—

In a deserted space in Mauritania, not far from the coast, the migrants themselves build the small boats to which they entrust their lives. It's a hidden, arid place, and so flat that it seems to stretch on forever. A few scraggly weeds are the only vegetation for miles. You can't see the ocean. You can't hear the ocean.

I arrived with Musa, Abbas, and his cousin Sadic, among others. Since Abbas was a member of an organization that had been operating in the smuggler hierarchy for years, he didn't pay to travel to Europe. That's how those networks operate: you slowly climb the ladder until they push you to make the trip. Abbas was an irritable man, and it didn't take much to spark his rage, but over time, I managed to gain his trust, and we became friends. I continued trying to befriend people older and more powerful than I was. I probably learned this skill as a little boy in Fiaso. It was the law of the jungle. The boys would fight on the walk to school to determine who was the strongest. One day, I picked a fight with one of the strongest boys. I definitely wasn't the strongest, but I was the most stubborn. We must have fought ten times on the way to school that day. I always lost, but I kept picking fights with him over and over again, until he finally gave in. We made peace and became friends. And because I was friends with one of the toughest boys in school, everyone respected me. And so I learned the benefits of befriending leaders.

Two dinghies were already being built when we arrived. There was a light-skinned carpenter in charge of construction, and the rest of us, Ghanaians and Nigerians, did whatever he told us: "Put a board over here, nail a board down over there." Then they brought us cans of black paint, and we brushed layer after layer onto the boats to make them waterproof.

We slept there too, even though there was no shelter. We just slept on the ground. Each of us choose a little plot of land and marked it with stones or branches, and that's where we put our belongings. It was sort of like having your own bedroom, even though it was just a slice of empty desert. When we first got there, they gave us plenty to eat, but as the days passed, our rations steadily decreased, until each of us had to make one loaf of bread last for three days.

There were nearly a hundred of us working there, and we were the lucky ones. Others were hidden away somewhere else, living in total uncertainty, unaware of what was happening or when we were going to leave. At least those of us building the dinghies knew roughly how long we would have to wait before we left. At our camp (if you could call it that), the Nigerians stood out because they were so religious: they were always reading their Bibles, and sometimes they would take breaks to pray. The atmosphere was generally upbeat. Once you've started down that path, all you can do is take things as they come. You have no other option: there's no turning back, no reconsidering your choices. And besides, we were on the final stretch of our journey toward achieving our dreams.

After a month, it was finally time to head for the coast. We felt a mix of joy and horror at the prospect of facing the sea. The smugglers made us all kneel and counted us over and over again. At night, they drove us toward the coast in cars with only one headlight on, or at some points with no headlights on. But it was all for show, because the police were almost certainly in league with the smugglers. A few kilometers before we reached the coast, the smugglers made us all get out and continue on foot. As we walked, we heard the sounds of the Atlantic, the constant murmur of crashing waves. When we reached the shore, our dinghies were there waiting for us. The smugglers lined us up and made us hand over all our belongings.

"In Europe you'll have everything you ever wanted," they told us, "so we'll keep this stuff; you won't be needing it."

They even made me give them a plastic watch I'd bought in Libya, which I had a certain fondness for. All I took was a bag with special clothes for when I arrived, and shoes with the laces tied together, which I slung over my neck. The smugglers divided us between two dinghies. Some migrants didn't fit, so they would have to wait for the next convoy; no one knew how many more weeks they would be in limbo.

They heaved the dinghy into the water, and right away, two Arab smugglers started placing us inside, one by one. I was the first one in because I was still pretty small: they had to lift me in their arms and place me inside. I curled up in a corner at the edge of the vessel. They put the women in next. Musa and I wouldn't see each other again until we reached the other side, because we ended up in different boats, but we didn't have a chance to say goodbye—in those circumstances, it's like being a soldier on the battlefield: people are yelling, and every step could make the difference between life and death. There is no time for sentimentality.

The sea was rough that night: it was windy, and the dinghy rocked from side to side. "The first three waves will be very strong, but don't worry, after that, it'll be calm all the way to Europe," they told us. "After those first waves, the surface of the water is so smooth you could play tennis on it."

They fit one hundred of us on the first dinghy, which was skippered by a light-skinned man who controlled the engine at the stern. After we were all in, we set off. It was true; the first three waves were extremely forceful, and powering through them in pitch-black was like riding a roller coaster: the nose of our small boat would rise higher and higher, then crash straight down, soaking everyone. In the distance, all we could see were a few lights on the horizon, small Mauritanian villages and roads. Everything else was dark. I thought we were going to die. I was genuinely afraid, clenching my teeth and praying.

But what they told us was true. After we'd gotten past the third wave, the sea became less tumultuous, and the farther we traveled from shore, the calmer it got, even though sometimes a wave would rock us from side to side and I'd get a mouthful of salt water. I couldn't see anything: I had no point of reference except for the stars overhead, which the captain used to navigate.

After several minutes with no sign of the other dinghy, we stopped to wait. The captain called the other smugglers on his cell phone to see what had happened. Apparently, the second dinghy was having mechanical troubles and we should continue without them. The captain responded in Arabic that in that case, he should be paid more since he was taking on additional risk alone. The two parties started to negotiate then and there, with our lives hanging in the balance.

It was extremely uncomfortable on the boat: we were packed so tight we could barely move. We had no life jackets, and none of us knew how to swim. No one said anything, we were terrified. The captain hung up and asked us:

"Do you want to die, or do you want to turn back?"

We all agreed we would rather turn back, so that's what we did. When we reached the shore, the waves capsized the boat and we fell in the water, but thankfully, it was shallow enough to stand. "Run, run!" the smugglers urged us. As we ran through the water, we saw the bodies of the passengers from the other dinghy. They had lied to us: there hadn't been any mechanical troubles. The other dinghy had sunk. They didn't make it past those first three waves. No one on board could swim; all of them had died. They fell in the water and sank like stones. It was so dark they probably couldn't have even oriented themselves toward the shore. Most heartbreaking of all, it was shallow enough to stand just a few meters away. If they had known how to swim, and in which direction, they could have easily saved themselves. Somewhere among the corpses was my friend Musa.

For a long time, I felt guilty about his death. I was tormented by the idea that if I'd found him that night, I could have pumped the water out of his lungs and revived him. But I didn't. They yelled, "Run, run," and I ran. They brought us to a camp. We were overcome by a brutal sadness. Everyone kept their eyes on the ground. No one said a word.

—⁓—

We woke up to the smugglers shouting.

"Let's go, come on, let's go! Everybody up!"

The Moroccan authorities had discovered the bodies on the shore and had begun a search of the whole area. We were in danger. A helicopter was sweeping the coast, looking for us. So we rushed away from our encampment, and the smugglers hid us as best they could in a cave over one hundred meters deep. It was terrifying. The Nigerians hesitated outside, afraid.

"We're not going in there."

"You have no choice, go in there and get all the way to the back," the smugglers told them. "If you stay out here, they'll see us!"

The smugglers kept us there for several weeks; that cave became our home. They said if we even stepped outside, someone might discover us. Every three days, they came to check on us and bring us a few loaves of bread. We had nothing to do all day. Just sleep on the ground. Wake up. Stretch. Talk a little. Eat some bread. Go back to sleep. Day after day. Night after night. Looking at each other. This time, we were the ones forced to wait while someone else built the dinghies, and we had no idea how long it would take. No idea when we would finally try to cross the ocean again.

"We'll go tomorrow," the smugglers promised.

But the next day, they said the same thing, and nothing ever changed. Sometimes I thought we would stay there forever, trapped for the rest of our lives in this apprehensive, bored, drowsy state. One day, Sadic started crying:

"I don't want to go back on the ocean!" he cried. "I won't do it!"

"You've got to, there's no going back!" his cousin Abbas said.

After a while, Sadic said he could do it because he'd promised his mother that he would reach Europe. That kept him going.

Then one night, at nine, when it was already dark, we heard cars drive up. The smugglers came in and started shouting at us. They only ever shouted, like we were in the army and they were our sergeants. "Let's go, up! Everybody, let's go!" We had to gather everything quickly, then walk several kilometers to the coast, which was horrible because I had lost my shoes. When we made it to the beach, we were once again divided between two boats. At that point, after so much hardship, I felt that life had no value whatsoever. In the whole world, there's just you and the two options before you: reach Paradise alive, or die. There is no other choice. I don't know if I was afraid, but one man definitely was: he whimpered and refused to get in the dinghy, so the smugglers beat and insulted him.

"Coward! You've come this far, how could you give up now?!"

Finally, they managed to get him on board.

The waves were less choppy that time around, and we got away from shore without difficulty. The challenge came when we reached the open ocean: that was when the seas turned rough. It was a forty-eight-hour trip, though nobody had told us that beforehand.

"The sea is like a mountain," said our captain, a Black Gambian fisherman. "First, you've got to climb up one side. Then you let yourself fall down the other. No need for gasoline, you make it on inertia alone." It struck me as very strange.

It's impossible to relax on that voyage. You're constantly looking death in the face: you know a thousand things could go wrong at any moment, and any one of them could kill you. We didn't have life vests, just a little Coca-Cola, some bread, and a few tins of sardines to pass around. When the dinghy took on water, Abbas was supposed to bail it out, but he got so tired that he couldn't heave the water overboard, and it fell back inside the boat. He was utterly exhausted.

The sea was fairly tame during the day. It was strange to be in such a small boat in the middle of nothing. It was the desert again, but made of water this time. The ocean was all around us; there was nothing on the horizon. I prayed and talked to myself, begging my family to forgive me if I died on that voyage, so close to my destination. I apologized over and over again, knowing I could die at any moment.

At one point, we saw an enormous ship in the distance, and we debated whether it was worth approaching. The captain said it was too dangerous: the wake of a ship that big could capsize us. We let it slowly pass, unsure if we were heading in the right direction or if we'd become lost in the immensity of the sea, a speck of dust in the middle of the vast ocean.

As the sun set, things went from bad to worse. The waves grew to the size of monsters and threatened to crush us. Sometimes they genuinely looked like vertical walls that our rickety dinghy had to climb. I was afraid we would sink. Everything was a dense, deep blue color, and each wave had a different shape. One instant we were elevated above it all, and the next, we were plummeting down, sure to be trapped between the waves . . . I was terrified. It felt like a horror movie.

SPAIN

"Look! Look!" someone cried out on the second night of our voyage. "A light!"

Everyone's heart leaped. Was there really a light? Was there dry land ahead? We gazed intently as the captain oriented us toward it. The waters had become choppy again, and I wondered if we would sink so close to our destination. It was agonizing.

Suddenly, we heard a helicopter overhead. The captain turned off our motor so they wouldn't hear us, but there was no hiding: they shined a spotlight straight on us. I could feel the helicopter blades churning above the dinghy. I thought they were going to rescue us, but when they flew off, my anxiety returned. I still don't know if they decided to ignore us or if it was the police and they were alerting others about our arrival.

We continued toward the light, which never seemed to get any closer, until, little by little, we began to see the other lights, the typical glittering rows you always see on the coastline. After what seemed like an eternity, we approached a rocky region. Thankfully, it was a beach and not a steep cliff where it would have been impossible to make landfall. I couldn't help but imagine how frustrating that would have been: to spend five years on a torturous journey through Africa only to die literally crashing into Europe.

The dinghy landed heavily on some rocks. Our captain hadn't tried to take us ashore in a calmer, safer area because we were almost out of gasoline. For the last several hours, he had been turning the engine on and off, riding the current when he could, and only burning fuel when he had no other choice, using as little as possible. We had almost none left by the time we arrived.

Our boat capsized when we ran into the rocks, and many of us fell overboard. I was thrown into the water, disoriented; I thought I was going to die like Musa, sinking like a stone because I didn't know how to swim. My legs were numb after two days crammed into a dinghy with a hundred other people, but when I finally managed to unbend them I touched the ground. I pushed up with both feet as the current jostled me this way and that. It took a few tries, but finally, I managed to get my head above water. I could breathe. I had survived. And at long last, I was in Paradise. When I reached the shore, I threw myself against the ground and hugged it with all my strength: I was safe, on dry, stationary land.

Abbas had a phone, and his first act on European territory was to climb the rocks and make a phone call, I assume to Rajman.

"Tousa! Tousa!" he cried, which means something like "we did it." It's what you say after you score an incredible goal in soccer. Everyone was throwing themselves onto the beach, lifting their hands to the heavens, giving thanks to God.

I felt helicopter blades above our heads again. I didn't know who they were, but they left almost the instant they saw us. Again, I wondered if it was a police helicopter sending notice of our arrival. In any case, some aid workers soon came to collect us. I'll never know if anyone drowned when we capsized against the rocks. There had been a woman with a baby, but I didn't see them when we reached the shore. We walked to the road, where the Red Cross and police were waiting for us, handing out blankets. I didn't see the child anywhere. I didn't see a body either.

—⁓—

After reaching land, we had walked toward the nearest lights. There, the police took our names; there were also journalists with cameras and flashlights, and a general sense of commotion. I was the last one to talk to the police. They put me in a comfortable car, gave me food and water, and drove me to the doctor, who took my vital signs and gave me a quick checkup.

I was happy because suddenly someone with no ulterior motives was taking care of me. The difference between this and the way I'd been treated by the smugglers was jarring. These white people even welcomed us with a certain amount of kindness: they smiled, spoke to us in a friendly tone, and asked us questions about our journey and how we were feeling. It was true: Paradise was a wonderful place.

Throughout this whole process, I had a bag hanging around my neck with the good clothes I had saved to wear in Paradise. The Red Cross workers made us shower, throw out the clothes we were wearing, and put on tracksuits they gave us, but I managed to hide my special clothes and wear them underneath.

Where were we? I didn't know. I just knew that I was in Paradise, in the Land of the Whites, on the other side of the ocean. They told me I was in a country called *España*, on an island called Fuerteventura, part of the Canary Islands. I had thought Paradise was all one big country. I had never heard of *España* before. The only words I heard that sounded slightly familiar were *Spain* and *Barça*.

"How old are you?" they asked me at the Red Cross center.

"I don't know," I answered. "I know I was born on a Tuesday."

Apparently that information wasn't very useful. I asked some other migrants how old they were, to try to get an idea by comparison. For example, one boy who was much bigger than

I was said he was fourteen. I thought, "There's no way that I'm older than a boy as tall as that," so I said I was fourteen too, even though I had no idea.

After we had been identified, they brought us to the police station, which was a very different place, full of tall, burly, unkind men. I was afraid of them. They were brusque when they talked to us, and they told us we couldn't bring anything into the country; even so, they didn't force me to take off the precious clothes I was wearing under my tracksuit. I think people turned a blind eye since I was still just a kid.

—ℳ—

From the police station, we were brought to an immigration detention center. It was a low, white building, surrounded by barbed wire and dry, neglected land. By the door, a flag was flying with two horizontal red stripes and one thicker yellow stripe in the middle. It was the first time I'd ever seen the Spanish flag. After we went through several inspections, they admitted us to the center and led us to a hall full of bunks. It was big and echoey, like an industrial warehouse. They made us shower, assigned us beds, and gave each of us soap, toothpaste, and a blanket. We slept through our first night, and early the following morning, they rang a loud bell: it was time to get up. They lined us up like soldiers, then gave us prepackaged pastries and coffee for breakfast. We were usually pretty hungry in the detention center: they fed us, true, but never enough. Milo, another migrant, shaved everyone's head because we all had lice. He also plucked dozens of splinters and other things out of the soles of my feet, which were black as tar. I'd lost my shoes after that first, failed attempt to cross the Atlantic and had been barefoot ever since. I'd lost all feeling in my feet.

You can't see anything from inside the detention center; you're completely walled in. Even so, it felt like a five-star hotel to me, especially compared to the places I'd been living: the floor of a desert cave, the cramped apartment in Casablanca, the Libyan brothel. Here, I had a bed all to myself. Later, living in Spain, I learned that the place is considered a prison. I never imagined that I'd find myself in a place like that after reaching Paradise.

One of the guards at the detention center was always very rough with us. Maybe it was to make sure we respected her since she was a woman and most of us weren't used to seeing women in positions of authority. Whenever she was the one to line us up, she hit us with her baton, even though almost everyone was cooperative and obedient. If you said anything, she hit you. There was no reason for her to be so brutal with us. We were scared whenever she was on duty.

We didn't know anything: not where we were, not why we were there, and not how long we would stay. To keep us busy, we were sent to the yard with wheelbarrows and tools to dig water trenches and do other kinds of maintenance work. We ate breakfast, lunch, and dinner. We worked. And when they let us, we played soccer. The tasks for inmates in that kind of place are extremely basic: cleaning, serving food, gathering the dishes. The people who had been in detention the longest did the most work.

There were also hustles in the detention centers, little favors you could do to get them to put extra food on your plate. Typical prison stuff. Even though the environment wasn't as hostile as a criminal prison, people did tend to form groups that were based, among other things, on whether they were from former British or former French colonies. There were absurd stereotypes, like the idea that migrants from English-speaking countries are smarter than the French speakers because we were part of the British Empire, which conquered the world. They're absurd preconceived notions that don't have any basis in truth, but they circulate all the same. One thing was true, though: the French speakers did tend to have more money. Their currency was more valuable than ours, so they had managed to save more before coming to Spain. Me, I didn't have a penny, though I don't know what I would have done with money anyway: you couldn't buy anything at the detention center except for telephone cards. Some migrants would steal fruit from the canteen and sell it to the French speakers. Hierarchies took shape between those walls. And all the while, I didn't even know there was a chance they might send me back to Africa. I wasn't worried.

One day, the staff brought me to a building where they took photos of me, asked me questions, and put my wrists against a machine. They took X-rays to try to determine my age by looking at my joints. They concluded that I was seventeen years old. Since I was still a minor, international law said I had the right to remain in the country. Every three days, they would put me in a small, private interview room and ask me the same set of questions over and over again. You would be sitting in the dark when, suddenly, you would hear someone asking you things, often in your own language:

"What's your name? Who is your father? Who is your mother? Where are you from?" the voice would ask in English.

I think they kept making me go to these interviews to see if I would lie or contradict myself. Once, a friend of mine named Yima Nkoranza came out with a black eye, and I think it was because they hit him for lying. He was Nigerian, but he was trying to pass as Ghanaian. Based on international agreements, if they thought he was from Ghana, there was a better chance they'd let him stay. At one point, he had been stuck in a smuggler camp, and while he was there, he had learned to speak Twi, one of Ghana's forty-two languages.

After a month, I was released from the detention center. Since I was seventeen, they recognized my right to remain in Spain. They said they were sending me to Málaga, which I thought was great, even though I didn't know what or where Málaga was. They handcuffed me and fourteen others and took us outside, where we were escorted by police with huge guns. I was surprised—based on how heavily they were armed, you would have thought we were dangerous criminals or terrorists. It reminded me of being caught in Algeria. They brought us to the airport, put us on a small plane, and flew us to the mainland. In Málaga, we took a van to another immigration center with police at the door, where they finally removed our handcuffs.

I was there for only three days. The difference was that at this center, the door was open. We could come and go as we pleased, then come back to sleep at night. They told us we were free.

"¿En qué lugar de España te gustaría vivir?" an agent asked me from across a table one day.

She gestured to a map of Spain that was hanging on her wall.

"Spain?" I suggested.

"Sí, Spain, Spain*; ¿en qué lugar de* Spain *quieres vivir?"* she asked.

I had no idea where in Spain I wanted to live. I didn't even know the names of any cities. Suddenly, my mind went back to those evenings watching soccer on TV in Accra.

"Barça?" I ventured, thinking of the soccer team.

"Ah, Barcelona."

She laughed, but sent me there anyway. And that's how I ended up living in Barcelona. Sometimes, the smallest detail in the present can determine your entire future. They gave me a train ticket, a water bottle, a banana, and a tuna sandwich, as well as a document saying I was number 101. That reminded me of the concentration camps I had seen in World War II movies. I want to believe they gave us numbers because our names were hard for them to pronounce, but I'd like to know for sure one day.

That was all I had as I started a new life.

—⟋⟋⟋—

When I woke up, the sun had already risen; I had slept through the night aboard the train. My body ached from sleeping in an unnatural position, and I really had to pee, but I didn't know that there are bathrooms on Spanish trains, so I'd held it for the entire trip. When I was growing up, there were no trains in Ghana.

When I got off the train and set foot in my new city of Barcelona, I felt an overwhelming sense of happiness. Then, instantly, I felt fear, because I found myself face-to-face with an escalator, something I had never encountered before: I thought it looked like an enormous, deadly python. Everything was new and exciting. And there were countless aspects of this new world that I didn't understand. This, at last, was Paradise, the Promised Land. It was February 24, 2005.

I walked along the streets and looked at the houses, which I thought were extremely tall. I took in all the trees and the different colors, trying to get a feel for the climate and find my bearings. That first day in Barcelona, I just wandered around, gazing at my surroundings, astonished, looking at everything as if I were unwrapping a gift over and over. I stopped in a park to watch some kids play soccer. The whole environment was so different: everything was beautiful and peaceful. Abundance everywhere. And I was free to do whatever I liked. I was elated.

But there was a flip side to that freedom: I had nowhere to sleep, I didn't know anyone, and I couldn't speak the language. I was starting from scratch. As I walked down the street, I said hello to everyone I passed, which is the custom in my country, but no one replied. Many people looked perplexed, as if it were ridiculous for me to speak to them.

"These white people are so strange!" I thought. "What are they afraid of?"

Later, I learned that it's not common for people to greet strangers on the street in Spain. At night, I used my six euros (which the agent in Málaga had given me) to buy some pastries and a soda at a bakery. I wasn't off to a good start: I'd had one meal, and already my pockets were nearly empty.

I ended up sleeping in a neighborhood called Navas. I didn't stop there for any particular reason; it was just where my meandering walk had led me. I tried to sleep at the entrance to a park, but every time I heard a car, I got scared and ran off.

On my journey through Africa, I'd had to be on guard at all times, and my body was still reacting as if I were in constant danger. I was in the habit of being on the alert, even though that wasn't as necessary in Spain. Since it was very cold (it was February), I jumped around every once in a while and did other exercises to warm myself up. Then I would lie down and try to fall back asleep.

The next day, as I was sitting on a bench, I felt a curious, inexplicable urge. It was like a voice telling me, "Ousman, get up and speak to that woman walking by. She will be able to help you."

I followed the woman down the street until she became aware of my presence and turned around. She didn't understand when I spoke to her in English, so she grabbed my hand and pulled me away from the foot traffic. Then, she called her husband, who spoke some English. He asked me question after question, including, once again, how old I was.

"I was born on a Tuesday."

I explained who I was and what I had been through. I had just arrived in Barcelona the day before, I was lost, and I didn't know anyone there.

The woman's name was Montse, and her husband was Armando. I have no idea what drove me to stop her and not any of the other people on the street that day. Later, I learned it was a cosmic coincidence. She lived in the suburbs, in Sant Cugat, and almost never walked around in Barcelona. She usually drove, but that day, for some reason, she had decided to take the metro. And she was almost never in Navas; she owned a shop in Barcelona, in the Gràcia neighborhood, which was all the way across town. She was only in Navas that day because her son had a small business there, and she was dropping by.

Montse took me to a nearby café and bought me breakfast. There was a bathroom in the café, thank goodness: I hadn't wanted to pee on the street—I was afraid something bad might happen if I got caught. Now that I had made it to Paradise safe and sound, I didn't want to ruin everything over something as silly as a full bladder. In Paradise, people don't even spit on the street, much less pee on it. I didn't want them to put me on a plane back to Ghana. I had to behave myself.

After using the bathroom, I was more relaxed. I was settling back into my chair just as the waiter arrived with our food. Montse drew a map of how to get to the Red Cross, then walked with me to the metro and bought me a ticket. She gave me her phone number, and even though we didn't have a common language, she made me understand that she didn't want me to sleep on the street again, because it was very cold.

—m—

The first hurdle I had to overcome was my fear of the enormous python that was the escalator. I remember that, far-fetched as it seemed, I wasn't too surprised to learn there was a train that ran underground. Everything was already surreal, it was like living in an imaginary world, and I was getting used to it. But I still didn't understand the concept of the metro: I had no idea that this tunnel full of people and trains formed a network that stretched underneath the entire city, or that you could use it to travel all over Barcelona. On the train, I watched the other passengers carefully to learn how they behaved in that underground labyrinth.

I headed toward the Plaça d'Espanya stop, clutching the handlebar, surprised by how the people of Paradise traveled, how they dressed. The women's clothes were particularly shocking. In Libya, you hardly ever saw women on the street, and you would never dream of speaking to them. They certainly didn't dress like European women. I met a Spanish woman on that first metro trip. I was on the platform at Plaça d'Espanya, trying to make the map Montse had drawn for me on a napkin line up with the metro map on the wall: it was impossible. I couldn't read, and I didn't understand all the different lines and symbols. Then I heard a female voice behind me. It felt strange to have a woman so close.

"Hola, ¿tienes problemas?" she asked. *"¿Te puedo ayudar?"*

Once she realized I didn't understand her, she started speaking English. I was a little flustered and confused by her spontaneous offer of help, and after learning to steadfastly avoid women in Libya, talking to her made me nervous. Speaking with an older woman like Montse was one thing, but I was worried about what might happen if someone caught me talking to this young woman in tights and a miniskirt. I told myself, "Ousman, you're not in Libya anymore. It's okay. This is a different continent, and nothing will happen to you if you speak to a woman." So I accepted her help. Her name was Eva and she was twenty-three. I quickly told her about my situation and said I was trying to go to the Red Cross. The only thing I had was a document saying I was number 101. I told her that I'd already been through migrant detention and was allowed to be in Spain.

"I'll take you. I have a South American friend who got here two months ago, and I know how the process works," Eva offered.

"If you say so . . ."

We got on a train together. Eva told me to sit next to her, but I stayed standing: I was afraid I might accidentally touch her. I probably looked her up and down a thousand times, but she was so cheery and talkative that my fear was beginning to fade.

"I want to be white," I told her. "I want to be an airplane pilot, and a doctor, and an engineer."

She laughed. "Really? All that?"

We spent the whole morning together. I told her about my dreams, the obstacles I had faced, and all kinds of other things. And we took my immigration document from office to office, but no one would help us.

"I think they suspect we're together, and that's not doing you any favors," Eva said.

"But aren't we together right now?"

"No, I mean together like a couple!"

After we got turned away from another government office, she told me she had errands to run, so I should go to the next one by myself to see if they could help me, or at least give me a place to sleep.

"Here," she said, "take my backpack. You'll need it more than I will."

She also gave my forty euros and her phone number.

"Just don't call until you're a doctor, engineer, or pilot!"

She told me she still lived with her parents. She was broke; there was nothing else she could do for me. But she promised that once I had established myself in Barcelona, we would celebrate together. "I'm sure that won't be long," I thought. "We'll have lots of fun."

―⊶⊷―

Meeting Montse and Eva had raised my hopes: there was humanity in this place, and I remained optimistic that one day I would be completely accepted, a full-fledged member of this prodigious society. It was comforting to know there are good people out there.

I started going to the EICA, a school where adult immigrants learn to speak Spanish and Catalan. They had a particularly hard time with me since besides not speaking Spanish, I could hardly read or write in any language. I was nearly illiterate: in Ghana, I had gone to school for only two years. All I could do was read a little Arabic, because they taught us to recite around fifteen percent of the Qur'an from memory; I'll remember those verses until the day I die.

I was eager to go to school and learn, even though it was harder than I'd expected. My ideas about Europe had been extremely naïve: I'd assumed that everything would be easy, that I'd acquire knowledge almost by magic, or by using sophisticated technology that would manipulate the circuits in my brain to implant information in my head. But no, you have to work for it. I've always had a good ear for languages, and it only took me three months to speak Spanish and Catalan. I was making good progress with writing too.

Clara, the teacher and school director, taught us vocabulary by drawing objects on the board, then writing the object's name: *elefante, sombrero,* and so on, the same way you would teach children. I remembered everything, thanks to my photographic memory and my determination. I wanted to learn so I could survive and succeed in this new world. It turns out *elefante* wasn't too useful, because there aren't many elephants in Barcelona. I do see a *sombrero* every once in a while, though.

At the EICA, they told me if I wanted a place to sleep, I should go back to the Red Cross at Plaça d'Espanya, where Montse had tried to send me. I met a boy named Julio, who had just arrived from Argentina; he was a photographer, he spoke English, and he knew how to get to Plaça d'Espanya, so I stuck with him. From the Red Cross, they sent us to sleep at a sports complex in the Poblenou neighborhood. For the next few days, I clung to Julio: he was like my guide since I didn't know how to get around the city. He had a map and knew how to read it. We lived without money: studying at the EICA, eating at a Catholic soup kitchen, sleeping at the sports complex. Walking everywhere.

But after three nights, they said we couldn't continue sleeping at the sports complex, because it was open only during the coldest weeks of winter. Julio and I parted ways; I went back to spending my nights on the street. I walked from business to business looking for work, but most people didn't understand me, and the people who did understand me didn't want to hire me. I learned that when you come to Europe the way I did, it's easy to get trapped in a cycle of poverty and destitution. Starting a new life is hard when you're an African migrant who's still learning the language, with no friends, no education, and no money. You have nothing. I began noticing others like me everywhere, other migrants who had gotten stuck, like the sinkers I'd seen along my journey through Africa, though life in Spain wasn't as cruel as it was in Agadez or the Valley.

"There has to be a solution," I told myself, "some way for all the people who have just arrived to escape this grinding poverty." Later, I learned that this isn't a priority in Spain: the economy is saturated with immigrants working as day laborers, finding seasonal jobs picking fruit, and doing other low-paying jobs that Spaniards don't want.

Now that I was back on the streets, I tried to sleep close to the school. Barcelona felt like an urban jungle: I didn't know where anything was, and I had to spend the nights outside. Supposedly there were shelters and soup kitchens, but everything was written in a language I couldn't understand. The documents and instructions they gave me at the Red Cross were incomprehensible. I was helpless. One day, a well-dressed Black man approached me as I was sitting on a bench. He spoke English:

"Are you hungry?" he asked.

I said yes, and he took me to lunch at a restaurant in the Barceloneta neighborhood. He was from Senegal, and he said he was very established in Europe because he'd lived in Belgium for ten years. He asked me to come with him on the train to a town outside Barcelona. Before I knew it, we were in Puigcerdà, on the border with France. He brought me to a house where several Senegalese men lived together. One of them was more arrogant, and he seemed to be the one who called the shots. He had his own laptop and said he was a rapper or something. The others were more normal, just regular guys, religious. The leader promised me work: he would give me money to buy merchandise, which I could then sell on the street. I think he was also involved in selling marijuana. He said he would sort everything out for me.

Sometimes, life puts you in strange situations. That night, while I was sleeping, the man who had brought me to Puigcerdà forced himself on me sexually. He tried to rape me. I resisted, and he was afraid that I would wake the others up and they would see what was happening. I ended up sleeping on the floor.

We didn't talk about it the next morning; we just ate breakfast as if nothing had happened, then left the house and caught the train. The final destination was Barcelona, but he said we had to get off earlier, at another town on the outskirts of the city. On the way, he promised that he wouldn't try to force himself on me again, that he would treat me with respect. I said okay. At the stop he'd mentioned, he said, "Here we are, come on."

"No," I answered. "I'm staying on."

"Get off! This is our stop!"

"No, I'm continuing to Barcelona."

He tried to pull me off, and we struggled a little, but there were other people on the train, so he let me go. He didn't want to attract attention. And in any case, he didn't have much time, because the doors were closing. He got off and I stayed on.

Another time, I was sitting in a park, and a woman started trying to speak to me in Spanish. We couldn't understand each other very well, but she went to her house and came back with her daughter, and they offered me some croissants. They were from Equatorial Guinea, a former Spanish colony in Africa. After a while, a well-dressed man showed up: the daughter's husband. They were very young, but already married with children.

"You don't know anyone here?" they asked.

"No," I answered. "I don't know anyone in Europe. I'm completely alone."

They brought me to their house, where they all lived together, and I took a shower. That night, I began to sob: I was so sad I couldn't help it.

"Don't worry, don't cry," said the daughter's husband. "You're safe here. It's all right. Come on, let's go out tonight."

He loaned me some nice clothes, and we met up with some of their friends to go to a Guinean nightclub. More and more people kept showing up, and everyone was dancing. It was a great party. They told me I should talk to some girls. "Are they joking? I'm in no condition to flirt," I thought. Still, I tried to go with the flow, and I ended up having a good night. As we walked back to their house, my new friend and his wife quarreled the whole way. I slept on their couch. They hosted me for three days, but we could barely communicate: I still couldn't speak Spanish, and their English wasn't very good. They started asking around, trying to find someone from Ghana. Eventually, they connected me with a Ghanaian friend of a friend named Erik. I went to meet him in the outskirts of the city, in Torre Baró. He invited me into his house, which had three bedrooms, two of which he rented to others. I stayed for a while, but eventually I had to leave to make room for Erik's wife.

After that, I spent a few weeks going to class, wandering the streets, and jumping the turnstile to ride the metro. At this point, I had no real goal: I was depressed, and I'd gone back to sleeping on the street. What had been the point of all this? Had I made such a long, dangerous journey only to end up homeless and alone? Then I remembered Montse; she had said to call her if I was ever in dire straits. I decided it was time to call.

A teacher at the EICA helped me send Montse a text message, because I could never have done it on my own. At the end of the message, I signed my name: Ousman. After a few minutes, I sent a second message explaining who I was, in case she didn't remember. I said that a month earlier, she had bought me breakfast and given me directions to the Red Cross. I said she was the only friend I had. After a few minutes, she answered: the next day, I should go to Plaça de Catalunya. Her husband, Armando, would meet me there. I didn't know what Plaça de Catalunya was, but when I saw it, I realized that

I walked past it every day. I felt so absurd. I didn't know how I would recognize Armando.

"Just wait there and you'll find each other," Montse had texted me.

So I stood at Plaça de Catalunya at the time she told me. And it's true, it wasn't hard for us to find one another, even though there were tons of people there (it's one of the most popular meeting places in Barcelona). Armando arrived and we exchanged a glance, each searching for a look of recognition in the other's eyes. He approached and asked if I was Ousman. And I was, in fact, Ousman. He said Montse would join us later.

He took me to lunch at a KFC, and I think I ate my own weight in fried chicken. Armando was a serious but kind-hearted man. We had a long conversation about all the set-backs I had experienced. He said that before he retired, he had worked as an engineer and a salesman, and Montse owned a shop in the Gràcia neighborhood that sold underwear, pajamas, that kind of thing. I showed him all my documents, including the certifications from the courses I had taken—to become a painter, a construction worker, even a tiler—to prove that I wanted to learn, to integrate. To prove that I had the right attitude. Among all my papers, he found one that said I had been assigned a lawyer at the Red Cross. There were so many documents I hadn't known which was which.

The next day, they said, we would go to the Red Cross because the lawyer was the person who could really help me.

—⁂—

I got there early. I brought my books and notes from class so I had something to distract me and keep me from getting too nervous while I waited. When Montse and Armando arrived, we went into the lawyer's office together. Montse was the exact opposite of her serious husband: she was bubbly, optimistic, and extroverted. She told me everything would turn out fine in the end. We spoke to a lawyer and a caseworker. The caseworker explained that I had two options. The first was to get a birth certificate from Ghana in order to prove that I was really seventeen years old. The Spanish government would be obligated to take charge of me until I turned eighteen, but the tests the doctors had given me in detention weren't good enough. Of course, I didn't have a birth certificate, it didn't exist; they don't issue documents like that in Ghanaian villages.

The other option was for Montse and Armando to adopt me and become my legal guardians until I turned eighteen. They didn't even hesitate. Like a miracle, they simply decided that they would do it. The moment they agreed, the caseworker began to cry. "I've never seen anyone do something like this," she said between sobs.

It was amazing, incredible news, though I have to admit that it also made me nervous: What if this wonderful couple was actually trying to take advantage of me somehow? I still didn't really know them. After witnessing and enduring so much vile exploitation on my journey, I was naturally suspicious of everyone. But they turned out to be just as they appeared—trustworthy and kind. Later, when I asked why they decided to help me, a complete stranger, they told me it was simple: they hoped someone would do the same if their own children were in my situation. Whether you call it luck or divine intervention, there is no doubt that from the moment I was born under a curse—when any other child from my tribe would have been left to die—fate has intervened to keep me alive. To me, it feels miraculous that I am where I am now, healthy, loved, and able to give back to the world. Maybe I did reach Paradise after all. Of all the miracles that brought me to this place, the one that brought me to Montse and Armando feels the most miraculous—and yet it is simply the miracle of human kindness.

Montse and Armando kept a vacant, rent-controlled apartment because it wasn't very expensive. I stayed there for a week or so, until we received the official notice stating that they would become my legal guardians. The apartment had three bedrooms; since I didn't know where to sleep, I chose the smallest one. I wanted to take up as little space as possible.

On my first morning in the apartment, I got some tape and began repairing the wallpaper, which the last tenant's dog had started tearing off the wall. I fixed it up as much as I could before going to my language class. That afternoon, Montse came by to give me a bag of clothes, and she was touched to see the small improvement. I think that was when I fully won her trust; in fact, I learned later that she called Armando after she left to tell him they would have nothing to worry about, I was a good kid. I hadn't done it to win brownie points or anything; I had just noticed that something was damaged, so I fixed it. That's all.

—⁓—

It felt like a scene from a movie: there were four judges, a lawyer on each side of the room, Montse and Armando, and me. I was extremely intimidated. "They organized all this for me," I thought. One of the judges solemnly read a text asking if I agreed to be Spanish and join this family.

"Spanish? No," I answered. "I want to be Catalan."

Of course, I had no idea that there was a conflict between the Spanish government and Catalans who want to be independent from Spain. I wanted to be Catalan because my family spoke Catalan, not Spanish, and I wanted to be part of my family. I didn't have any political motivation. As if we were talking about Walas and Dagombas, it seemed strange to me that if my parents were from the Catalan tribe, they would make me become part of the Spanish tribe.

Imagine: a seventeen-year-old boy, recently arrived from Ghana, in a Spanish courtroom, saying he wants to be Catalan. It was so strange that everyone fell absolutely silent. No one moved a muscle. As the seconds passed, I realized that I must have said something extremely offensive. But after a few moments of seemingly endless silence, astonishment, and confused looks, people's lips began to curve upward, and soon everyone in the courtroom was laughing.

"Sorry, kid," the judge told me. "For now, Spanish is the best we have to offer. Take it or leave it!"

"I'll take it, of course, of course!"

—m—

After my parents had formally adopted me, they had a party to celebrate and to introduce me to the rest of the family. That was the first night I spent in their house. Once the party was over, my mother showed me to the bedroom she had prepared, where she tucked me in as if I were a small child: she cocooned me in blankets, kissed my forehead, turned off the light, and closed the door behind her. I lay there in the silent darkness. Something confusing was happening: I was extremely upset.

I had hot water, a warm home, all the food I could eat, and a queen bed all to myself. But even though I was so comfortable on the outside, on the inside, a storm was raging. The world was collapsing around me. For the first time since leaving Ghana, I was safe. No more fighting to survive. My future wasn't uncertain. I was safe.

I started crying like a child. I lay there the whole night, wondering why I'd had to experience so much suffering. It says in the Qur'an that all things are predestined. And here I was in Barcelona, with this family that was prepared to love me selflessly, unconditionally, just the way I am, just for the sake of loving me. Had these people been here all along, waiting? Was this part of God's plan? If so, why had he placed so many obstacles on my path? Couldn't he have brought us together some other way? Couldn't he have brought them to Africa—on a safari, for example? What was the point in all that struggle? What was the point in all that suffering? Why did Musa have to die when we had seemed destined to be together? What crime had we committed? And why did I end up with this other fate? What had I done to deserve this?

HOME (SPAIN)

Now I'm Spanish, and I have a family.

At first, they thought it was strange when I called them *Mamá* and *Papá*.

"Mamá!" I'd say.

"Would you quit it with all this *'Mamá'* business?" Montse would answer.

But I loved being a part of their family, and it didn't take long before it would have felt wrong to all of us for me to call them anything else. It was a package deal: along with a mother and a father, I'd acquired two brothers, a sister, a niece, and a nephew. Joining the family was easy. I fit in perfectly: it felt like they were an incomplete puzzle and I was the missing piece. They welcomed me and loved me fully, without jealousy or inhibitions.

Oriol, the youngest of the siblings, was extremely proud to have an African brother. The first time he introduced me to his buddies was when they were having a party at someone's apartment. He had told them he was going to bring along his brother, and we had a lot of fun pretending not to notice their stunned reactions when he introduced me. He picked me up whenever Barça was playing (like I said, the team was the reason I'd ended up in Barcelona and not in Seville or Madrid), and I'd watch the game with him and his friends.

I continued living on my own in Gràcia, in the family's empty apartment, but I spent so many nights with my parents in Sant Cugat that I was practically there more than in the apartment. Meanwhile, I kept studying: I learned to read and write in Spanish and Catalan, earned my primary school equivalency certificate, started going to high school, and then got accepted into a university. I decided I wanted to study science because those were always the classes that I found most interesting. And all the while, I was working to pay for my studies. I'd finally gotten a job doing repairs in a bicycle shop.

—ᴍ—

I took classes in the evening so I could work during the day. Everything sparked my curiosity and I was eager to learn. Some nights, I couldn't even fall asleep because I was so excited about everything I would discover the next day. I don't think it's a very common feeling among students here, but I was eager to fill my mind with all the knowledge that I hadn't been able to access before. After all, it was exactly for this that I had set out on the journey out of my world eight years earlier.

Sometimes, I had to study in the evening after working all day at the bike shop, so I used a simple trick to keep myself awake: I'd put my feet in a bucket of ice-cold water. That kept me nice and alert, much better than coffee or other stimulants. It's impossible to fall asleep with your feet in cold water, even if you try.

When I was taking high school classes in the evening, most of my classmates were girls. There were only three boys. This was a unique experience for me because like I've mentioned, I wasn't used to being around women. The teacher often asked students to take attendance, and when it was my turn, I struggled with all the names in Catalan. It was awful. My classmates always made fun of me, laughing at me. If I had been white, they would have seen my face turning red with embarrassment. One day, I couldn't take their mockery anymore. I got very upset, and I scolded them in English.

"What do you think you're laughing at?" I shouted. "I'd like to see you try to read something in my dialect, in Wala, or in Ashanti! Then I'd be the one laughing!"

That shut them up. They hadn't expected me to lash out at them, but also, their English was very poor, and they may not have understood what I said. Still, I won their respect. Later, they voted unanimously to make me class president.

I was completely fascinated by natural phenomena. During my second year of *bachillerato*, which would be like senior year of high school in the US, we did a chemistry experiment in the lab, where we analyzed acetylsalicylic acid (aspirin). We had to draw the molecule and identify how it reduced headaches.

"I don't believe you about aspirin," I told our teacher. "You're trying to trick me."

"Trick you?"

"I've been tricked a lot in my life, but that's all over now, I won't be fooled anymore."

"But what is it that you don't believe?"

"Headaches aren't cured with aspirin. They're cured by my father's rituals."

We argued a lot, but the teacher, Luis, was very patient with me, even though I was so skeptical. He asked me how my father cured headaches, and I explained some of his shamanic rituals, which included using medicinal plants, lemon rinds, and pineapple peels. What I didn't know was that acetylsalicylic acid comes from the bark of the willow tree: even the term *salicylic* comes from *salix*, the Latin word for willow. I was fascinated. For my final project, I had wanted to analyze one of the plants that my father uses in his shamanic rituals, but my teacher said that was too complicated for high school.

Around that time, my teacher went to a pharmacology conference, where he met the directors of some pharmaceutical laboratories and companies. They were interested in what he told them about me, and eventually, he introduced us. They said I should study pharmacology in university because it clearly fascinated me. If I continued on that path, they would

130

give me lab space to analyze the plants my father uses, and they would even bring specimens from Ghana for me to study. I decided that was what I wanted to do: I would be a Western shaman, a pharmacist.

But my grades weren't good enough to be admitted into a pharmacy program, so I started studying chemistry instead, which was less competitive. At first, I had hoped to change programs after a few semesters, but I couldn't afford it. And in any case, the classes and labs conflicted with my work schedule. As an immigrant without a Spanish passport, I couldn't apply for public financial aid, and the degree programs aren't set up for students who have to work to make ends meet. Don't get me wrong, the education system in Spain is certainly better than Ghana's; otherwise, maybe I could have studied there. But Spanish universities have their problems too.

I loved studying the atom and other scientific concepts, and if I'd had the time, the background, and, most importantly, the money, I would have continued studying science. I found photosynthesis astonishing: I couldn't get over the idea that energy can never be created or destroyed, it just gets transformed in plants, and that's the basis for the survival of all life on Earth. How is it possible that light from the sun becomes the energy we get from eating a slice of bread? I'm wild about science and engineering; they've always fascinated me. I was never the brightest kid in the class, but considering all my challenges, I always did my best.

Another aspect of life here that I could never wrap my head around was this idea of "vacation." I took time off work only when I had exams. Once, I went on holiday with a girl-friend, and it was really hard because I didn't know what I was supposed to do with myself. Why were we wasting time like that? I need food, I need clothes, but I don't *need* vacation. I didn't understand that I had the right to take time off work, and to be honest, I still don't totally get the point of doing nothing on purpose.

Life began to move quickly. I studied public relations and marketing, and I decided to start my own NGO. I didn't want other kids in Ghana to suffer like I did. It was clear to me that the best way to help them was through education, because ignorance was a big part of what led me down my path. I got a degree from the Esade Business School, which offers one of the best MBA programs in the world. I hadn't won the lottery (I was still repairing bikes), but I convinced them to give me a scholarship because it would help me run my NGO.

"I'm not here to ask you for a million euros," I said in the interview. "I simply think that I have an obligation to reach more lives through my NGO, NASCO Feeding Minds. Studying here will better equip me to reach young people in Ghana so that they don't have to set out on the same terrible journey that I took."

"I've worked in this sector for many years," the admissions officer said, "and I've reviewed many applications, but yours is unlike any I've seen before."

He said that if I could juggle the degree program and working at the bike shop, they would give me a scholarship. I couldn't do it that year, because I still hadn't finished my undergraduate studies. The next year, they held the program in Madrid, not Barcelona, and I couldn't afford to move. But the third time was the charm, and now I have my MBA.

I was lucky to be in the right place at the right time. There is no doubt in my mind that I'm one of the luckiest people in the entire world, if only because I'm alive and present, here and now. I will never stop being thankful for that. I'm also so fortunate to have met so many people who have helped me achieve these ambitious goals, which otherwise would have been unimaginable for me. I fully recognize that I wouldn't have reached this point in life without the support of countless others.

When I think of the place I was born, the places I traveled through, and the place I now call home, I am struck by how completely different they all are. Three different cultures, three entirely different realities: first the Ghanaian jungle, then the Arab world, and finally Europe. In order to get from there to here, I had to learn how to navigate each one, and now I am in a position to see all of them at once, compare them to each other, and understand the advantages and disadvantages of each. This has given me a unique and slightly strange worldview—sometimes it helps me, and sometimes it gets in my way. Given all the hardship I've experienced, it would be easy to think that the world is full of bad people, but I prefer to think that most people are good. It's just that the good people make less noise.

AFTERWORD

They do something in Ghana that, from a European perspective, could seem both peculiar and sad. Students learn how to use computers at school, but without actual computers in the classroom. The teacher draws everything on a chalkboard: the monitor, the icons and menus, the keyboard, the mouse, and so on. They teach Excel by drawing entire spreadsheets by hand. Students have to learn to use computers to pass the university entrance exams, but many Ghanaians won't use these lessons until they see a computer. Some of them never will.

At my NGO, NASCO, our motto is "Feeding Minds," and our goal is to equip rural schools with computers, projectors, monitors, and everything else they need to teach students to use computers properly. Hands-on learning is the best kind of education. This is our small contribution to improving conditions in Ghana and solving the issue of migration at its source. The overall goal of NASCO Feeding Minds is to improve the situation in Ghana so that young people don't feel the need to migrate to Europe. I don't want anyone else to suffer like I did on my journey; no one should have to die traversing the desert or crossing the ocean. And to me, the best way to achieve this is through education, which is essential to satisfying children's curiosity and fulfilling their eagerness to learn. We believe that, ultimately, education is critical to a country's development. I began thinking about my NGO in 2010. After spending two years mulling it over, testing out ideas that didn't work, and having some small successes and small failures, I finally came up with a concrete plan. First, I asked for assistance from the Ghanaian government, but I didn't have much luck. I realized I would have to fund the project myself, so I taught myself how to write a project proposal. I was inspired by a crowdfunded bicycle repair project in London, and I started thinking that maybe crowdfunding was the best way forward. But that didn't pan out either: I didn't have the right contacts and wasn't very good at using social media. So a few friends loaned me some money, and I used my savings. I didn't have much, but it was a start. At the bank, they told me to be careful carrying all that money at once, and I laughed. They had no idea what I'd been through. If anyone understood how important it is to be careful with your money, it was me.

I returned to Ghana for the first time in 2012. Going back was hard; there was so much I didn't want to remember. My Spanish parents had suggested I visit my village shortly after I'd gotten my Spanish paperwork sorted out, but I didn't want

The Ghanaian village where I grew up is surrounded by lush vegetation. I had a happy childhood—I never went hungry—but my curiosity prompted me to set out for Europe, or, as I then called it, the Land of the Whites. In this photo: my older brother, Yakubu, with his two children, out gathering food. (From the personal archive of the author.)

When I was a kid, I would build my own toys. I was pretty good at making little cars and trucks. When I arrived in Europe, I was astonished to learn that children are given all sorts of intricate, expensive toys every year. In this recent photo of my village, a child is playing with a toy that looks just like the ones I used to make. (From the personal archive of the author.)

Every day, we walked seven kilometers to get to our school, which was no more than a few dozen chairs under a tree. If it rained, we went home. (From the personal archive of the author.)

Above and below: When I decided to leave for Europe, I had no idea that I would be traveling for four years, forced to trust my life to a patchwork network of smugglers. The journey led me to the Sahara, where I nearly died, and across the ocean, where I lost my best friend. I crossed the sea on a crowded dinghy very much like the one pictured below. After all that, when I finally reached the Land of the Whites, I realized it wasn't paradise after all: there too, I found myself alone, sleeping on the street. (Above: © TAG ID efesp-three068157/Album Archivo Fotográfico. Below: © EFE. TAG ID efesptwo532967/Album Archivo Fotográfico)

My first year in Barcelona. In the reflection, you can see my adopted parents. They welcomed me into their family as a son when I was seventeen, after I'd spent months on the street. They always say they hope someone would do the same if their own children were in my situation. (From the personal archive of the author.)

Me with my mother and niece on vacation, at a swimming pool near our campground. It's still hard for me to understand a "vacation" that involves leaving your home so you can sleep in a tent on the ground. If you ask me, luxury is a nice warm bed. (From the personal archive of the author.)

Fitting in with my new family was easy. It felt like they were an incomplete puzzle and I was the missing piece. After Armando and Montse took me in, I started calling them Mamá and Papá. (From the personal archive of the author.)

After everything I'd experienced, my first trip back to Ghana was difficult. My mother didn't even recognize me at first. This is a photo of me with the head of the tribe (left) and the spokesperson for the king of Fiaso (middle). (From the personal archive of the author.)

I was fortunate to meet Pope Francis at a special mass for refugees and migrants on June 6, 2018. (From the personal archive of the author.)

Whenever I look at this photo, it feels like I'm dreaming. I remember the boy from Ghana who could only respond "Barça" when asked where he wanted to live. When the president of FC Barcelona read that anecdote in the newspaper, he invited me to his skybox at Camp Nou Stadium. That day, I felt like I really had reached paradise. (From the personal archive of the author.)

The thought of returning to Barcelona from Ghana was also emotionally hard, since my original journey to Barcelona had involved so much suffering. The second time was much easier; I just took a plane. In this photo: two of my brothers, who took me to the airport. (From the personal archive of the author.)

Me with my parents. I'm very happy after getting my residence permit. (From the personal archive of the author.)

Above: These are children from my home village of Fiaso getting ready to go to school. Below: I'm just one of the millions of migrants who try to cross the border every year. The only thing that makes me different is that I was incredibly, miraculously lucky. Since reaching Europe, I have dedicated myself to education, trying to "feed the minds" of Ghana's children so that they never have to experience a painful journey like mine. (From the personal archive of the author.)

to. It was too painful. My father had died in 2008. We had spoken on the phone, but those were difficult conversations. I had a hard time explaining life in Barcelona to him; it was too much for my father to understand. He had never spoken on the phone before, and he was constantly shocked that the voice coming through this device was his son. "Ousman? Is it you?" He asked if I was surrounded by white men. I said yes. He asked what I was eating, always worried I didn't have enough food. We never really discussed anything beyond that. They weren't very profound discussions.

When I returned to my village, my mother didn't recognize me. I wanted to surprise her, so I made a plan with my younger brother. He and I talked regularly because he lived in the capital, so it wasn't as hard to get him on the phone. I was paying for his education. He told the family that some friends were coming to visit; some other friends of mine had passed through the village recently, so it wasn't hard to believe. I took a taxi to the village. When I got out, I wondered if anyone would recognize me. I didn't wear flashy clothes, just a gray T-shirt, shorts, and flip-flops. The only thing that stood out was my long, unkempt hair, which you almost never see in Ghana. It made me look like a hippie. It turned out I was the one who didn't recognize things: the village had changed completely since I'd left. Houses there burn down on a regular basis, and then they're rebuilt, sometimes in a different place. Plus, it rains heavily, and everything gets covered in mud. The village is constantly shifting. And I had been gone for a long time.

I crossed paths with my older brother, who had taken my father's place as shaman: he looked me up and down, then realized who I was. He was shocked to see me. He asked me what I was doing there, and I said I was trying to find my way back home. He led me to our house, but I asked him not to tell the rest of the family. When we arrived, my mother was doing some chores, hanging maize to dry on the patio. She had returned to Fiaso while I was traveling north. When my brother and I came in, she gave me a sidelong look and asked, "Who's this friend of yours with the weird hair?"

"He's one of my oldest friends, don't you remember?" he said.

She looked at me again, perplexed; I just stood there, acting casual. Suddenly, her face lit up as she recognized me. We hugged, and we both began crying. I had given her a lot of heartache, and she had really missed me.

I didn't have much time there, and I had a lot to do. Since it was my first return since the death of my father, I had to visit his tomb and sacrifice animals in several village rituals: it was a way of telling my father, who had moved on to the afterlife, that I had returned. Before he died, my father had promised that if I ever returned, he would give thanks to his gods. Even when everyone thought I had died on my journey, he clung to the hope that I was still living.

I was in Ghana for two weeks, but not just in my village; I also did some work laying the foundations for NASCO throughout the country. My brother, who was my partner on the ground, had tried to get the Ghanaian government to help us, but they didn't listen to him until I bought him a suit. In Africa, image is very important; people try hard to project success. If you don't, you'll never get far. It's something I've never liked. But in the end, the government is me, and the government is you; we're the ones in charge, and we have to continue forward. And that's what we did. It's like the famous saying that's sometimes attributed to Gandhi: "Be the change you wish to see in the world."

One of our first initiatives was in the Brong-Ahafo region, where I grew up. Like I said, it's one of the regions of Ghana that produces the most emigration. I spent $1,600 on permits, but after all the negotiations, and spending all that money, the school wouldn't sign the final papers to start the project.

Eventually, we managed to sign agreements with other schools. With my own savings and some money that my friends Gerard Muñoz and Laura Santaló loaned me, I purchased forty-five used computers; I bought them in Ghana to save on shipping, which can be very expensive. We took our computers to the Sawla-Tuna-Kalba District in the north of the country, and there we started our first computer lab at Saint Augustine Junior High School. That was where NASCO was truly born, on September 12, 2012. Thirteen hundred students from four different schools in the region have access to this computer lab, and the number of students who pass their university entrance exams has climbed from 52% to 71%. Since then, we have opened four more computer labs throughout the country and reached eleven thousand children.

There is a fee for all of this. The way I see it, if you offer something for free, people think it isn't worth anything. We ask students to pay a nominal amount to take classes. This way, they value it more. Not to mention, this way schools have some funds for repairs or other unforeseen circumstances. The cost is thirty cents per quarter.

I think that this is the best form of cooperation: not feeding bellies, but feeding minds. And always in collaboration with the local communities, which know their needs better than anyone else. That's what we do. Some nights, I fall asleep thinking about the eleven thousand children we have reached. If these efforts save just one of them from the experience I had, it will have been worth it. That is why I will continue to tell my story: so that one day, there are no more stories like mine to tell.

AUTHOR'S NOTE

I am aware that my story is an exception and that, of the hundreds of young people who set out on journeys like mine every day, most do not reach their destination. I was exceedingly lucky on my journey. Miraculously lucky. Now, I am trying to share that luck with the children in my country by equipping them with the tools and education they need to make informed decisions about their future. If you think that no one deserves to live through a story like the one you just read, I invite you to learn about NASCO's projects and, if you would like, to join in our efforts: https://nascoict.org/en/.

ACKNOWLEDGMENTS

My deepest thanks to Florencia Cambariere, literary director at Penguin Random House Argentina, and Xavier Grant for helping me make this book a reality. Without you, this would never have been possible. I would also like to thank Cesc Batlle and Francisco Rodríguez for the hours they took, probably from their night's sleep, to review the English translation from places as distant as New Zealand and London.

I'm profoundly grateful to my parents, Armando and Montserrat (Montse), for extending their help when I felt trapped at the bottom of a well, thinking I was the most invisible person in Barcelona. Thank you for giving me the chance to be reborn, for putting me on a different trajectory, for shining a light on my path in such a special way. Sometimes it's hard to believe that we've known each other for only thirteen years, especially when you say it feels like we've been together all our lives. I feel the same. I also want to acknowledge your humility, declining to appear in the media because you don't think you've done anything exceptional. I have nothing but gratitude for you.

A huge thank-you to my siblings for welcoming me into the family as a brother. Thanks also to Banasco Seidu Nuhu for listening to me and adopting my motto, which became our motto: *feeding minds*. Thanks for your strength and perseverance; I know all your efforts will pay off in the not-too-distant future. Thanks to Abdul Aziz Seidu for throwing his all into this opportunity. I know that you'll do incredible things.

I would also like to thank all the people and volunteers who have been essential to the creation and day-to-day operation of NASCO Feeding Minds, and especially Gerard Muñoz and Laura Santaló for their commitment and for loaning me the money to buy those first computers.

Particular thanks to all NASCO Feeding Minds volunteers and collaborators for their commitment and dedication, and especially for their trust and support during difficult times: Josep Maria Torné, David Lorenzana, Sonia Barahona, Daniel Pagés, Jordi Cegarra, the Martín family, the Pol Pau family, Ignasi Pi, Cristina Castells, Nagore Espanyol, Isabel Parelladas Basté, Mónica Massagué, Blanca Cegarra, Bet Garriga, Rosa Sitjà, Alba Pardo, Felix Capella, Blanca Molins, and Gisela Muxella.

Thanks to Mercè Espinosa, president of Mehrs, for loaning us office space at her company and for her personal support.

I would also like to thank some great friends who, from the shadows, have been doing incredible work to keep the NGO running: Eva Maria Vidal, Ferran Marqués, Ignasi Carreras, Jordi Ros, Jesús Giménez, Evaristo Aguado, Amparo Martinez, Buster Norsk, and especially Nuria Alegre for her concern and consummate professionalism when it was time to legally establish the NGO and for her selfless assistance with bureaucratic issues. I'm so grateful.

In 2018, besides making some wonderful friends, I also had the good fortune to meet people with incredible human warmth: Josep Santa Creu, Ignasi Pietx, Jordi Villacampa, Dr. Bonaventura Clotet, Raúl Ciprés from Creativialab, Miguel García, Susana Gembarowski, and all the others I can't name here. Thank you for your support, from the bottom of my heart.

I also want to acknowledge those friends who believed in me from the very outset: Gerard Muñoz, Laura Santaló, Ana Pallàs, David Marín, Cristina Goula, Montxo Dueso, Elena Álvarez, Roser Castellà, Mercè Martín Goula, Alan Taxonera, Dani González, Roger Sañé i Rius, Jordi Sirvent, and Joan Camacho. Thank you for all our wonderful experiences together.

I couldn't forget my friends the Castellers de Sant Cugat (Gausacs de Sant Cugat). You have helped me to do so much, including break stereotypes.

I'd especially like to thank Borja Xicoy for encouraging me to go to university when I didn't think that I could. I still remember when you brought me to the business school library. I was only studying Spanish and Catalan back then, but I was so dazzled by the university atmosphere. Thank you for inspiring me. Today, I can proudly say that I have my degree.

María Paloma, this book wouldn't be complete without your name: in your humble, quiet way, you have always loved me like a son. I will never forget your support when it came to paying for my studies.

Thank you, Koos Kroon, for giving me my first job in Spain. Besides being my boss, you are also a big brother to me. You always encouraged me to study and gave me all the assistance and flexibility I needed to work and study at the same time. You took a chance on me, and I would never have gotten my Spanish papers if it weren't for you. Thanks for all your support.

To all my teachers and professors:

Josep Maria Tanco: thank you for your patience, your constant motivation, and especially your dedication to helping me pass Spanish Literature, even when it meant long hours studying and private classes, even on Saturday nights. Thank you for your generosity and your help.

Eduardo Hernández: with you I saw snow for the first time, and I learned about photosynthesis and how important it is. Thank you for all the conversations on the existence of the universe.

Luis Serrado, chemistry teacher at the Institut Menéndez y Pelayo: thank you for your patience with all my questions, especially when I thought you were pulling my leg about aspirin alleviating headaches, because I believed magic was the only cure.

To my classmates: Alba Millán, Catalina Javiera, Jaume Gayard, Laura Liesa, Bernardo Santos, Carlota Bozal, Yvone Vila, Uri Roca, and Ferran Carbó, thanks to all of you for those long afternoons studying together.

ABOUT THE AUTHOR

Photo © Santi G. Barros

Ousman Umar was born in Ghana and immigrated to Europe when he was seventeen. In 2012 he founded NASCO Feeding Minds, an NGO dedicated to the principle that the most effective way to prevent migrants from leaving Ghana for Europe is to provide top-notch opportunities for education and advancement in Ghana. *North to Paradise* was originally published by Penguin Random House Spain in 2019. Ousman lives in Barcelona.

ABOUT THE TRANSLATOR

Photo © 2015 Maria K. Dunn

Kevin Gerry Dunn is a Spanish-English translator whose recent projects include *Countersexual Manifesto,* by Paul B. Preciado, and *Easy Reading,* by Cristina Morales (for which he received a PEN/Heim Translation Fund Grant and an English PEN Award), as well as works by Daniela Tarazona, Cristian Perfumo, and Kike Arnal. He also heads the FTrMP Project, an effort to make Spanish translations of vital migration paperwork available for free online.